Server Side development with Node.js and Koa.js Quick Start Guide

Build robust and scalable web applications with modern
JavaScript techniques

Olayinka Omole

BIRMINGHAM - MUMBAI

Server Side development with Node.js and Koa.js Quick Start Guide

Commissioning Editor: Amarabha Banerjee
Acquisition Editor: Reshma Raman
Content Development Editor: Smit Carvalho
Technical Editor: Sushmeeta Jena
Copy Editor: Safis Editing
Project Coordinator: Hardik Bhinde
Proofreader: Safis Editing
Indexer: Mariammal Chettiyar
Graphics: Alishon Mendonsa
Production Coordinator: Shraddha Falebhai

First published: November 2018

Production reference: 1291118

Published by Packt Publishing Ltd.
Livery Place
35 Livery Street
Birmingham
B3 2PB, UK.

ISBN 978-1-78934-539-1

www.packtpub.com

`mapt.io`

Mapt is an online digital library that gives you full access to over 5,000 books and videos, as well as industry leading tools to help you plan your personal development and advance your career. For more information, please visit our website.

Why subscribe?

- Spend less time learning and more time coding with practical eBooks and Videos from over 4,000 industry professionals

- Improve your learning with Skill Plans built especially for you

- Get a free eBook or video every month

- Mapt is fully searchable

- Copy and paste, print, and bookmark content

Packt.com

Did you know that Packt offers eBook versions of every book published, with PDF and ePub files available? You can upgrade to the eBook version at `www.packt.com` and as a print book customer, you are entitled to a discount on the eBook copy. Get in touch with us at `customercare@packtpub.com` for more details.

At `www.packt.com`, you can also read a collection of free technical articles, sign up for a range of free newsletters, and receive exclusive discounts and offers on Packt books and eBooks.

Contributors

About the author

Olayinka Omole is a software engineer currently based in London who grew up in Lagos, Nigeria. He is self-taught and primarily enjoys building with JavaScript, Python, PHP, and Java. He has written a lot about these technologies in multiple blogs and publications, including Sitepoint, and Scotch.io. He spends most of his time doing the usual fun things—writing code, learning how to write more code, and watching TV shows. His background in electrical and electronic engineering ensures that his passion for embedded engineering and DIY projects is also kept alive.

About the reviewer

Bhanu Pratap Chaudhary is a self-taught programmer who has been active in the JavaScript ecosystem for around five years now.
After working as a consultant, freelancer, engineer, lead, and CTO in various start-ups, he is working on an already profitable stealth-mode B2B start-up in the catering industry.

He can also be found boxing, listening to and writing music, and he loves to write simple and readable code.

Packt is searching for authors like you

If you're interested in becoming an author for Packt, please visit authors.packtpub.com and apply today. We have worked with thousands of developers and tech professionals, just like you, to help them share their insight with the global tech community. You can make a general application, apply for a specific hot topic that we are recruiting an author for, or submit your own idea.

Table of Contents

Preface

The release of modern versions of the JavaScript language has made it possible to build more modular and scalable applications in Node.js. Koa is a next-generation Node.js framework that has taken a lot of the newer JavaScript features to make development of robust web applications in Node.js much easier.

You will learn how to efficiently build robust web applications in Koa using modern paradigms and techniques in Node.js development.

Who this book is for

This book is for developers who are interested in building robust and scalable applications using Koa—a modern, expressive, and nimble Node.js framework.

What this book covers

Chapter 1, *Introduction to Koa*, introduces Koa and talks about its benefits for server-side web development. We will talk about the reasons why developers may choose to use Koa for software development. We will also introduce the remainder of the book and talk about how the book will help its readers to navigate the complex waters of Koa.

Chapter 2, *Getting Started with Koa*, explains how to get started with server-side development with Koa. We will learn how to install Koa, create a simple server, and build the obligatory *Hello World* app.

Chapter 3, *Koa Core Concepts*, discusses the application, context, and request and response objects in Koa. We will also learn about how to create and use middleware. We will go into detail about Koa's philosophy and show readers how the different parts of the framework work.

Chapter 4, *Handling Errors in Koa*, goes into error handling in Koa. We will look at the different methods of handling errors in Koa. The aim will be to make sure users have a solid foundation and know how to build Koa applications that don't break at slight exceptions.

Chapter 5, *Building an API in Koa*, dives into building a real-life application in Koa. We will show readers how to create routes, handle requests, and send responses from their APIs.

Chapter 6, *Building an Application in Koa*, reinforces what we will have learned by building a fully fledged web application in Koa. We will learn how to build a real-life application with authentication and structure it properly in Koa. We will also share some information on further reading to improve on the reader's knowledge of Koa.

To get the most out of this book

To get the most out of this book, having knowledge of JavaScript (ES6 syntax)would be beneficial.

Readers who want to use Koa in tandem with Node.js effectively in order to create fast and real-time backend applications will benefit from this book.

Download the example code files

You can download the example code files for this book from your account at www.packt.com. If you purchased this book elsewhere, you can visit www.packt.com/support and register to have the files emailed directly to you.

You can download the code files by following these steps:

1. Log in or register at www.packt.com.
2. Select the **SUPPORT** tab.
3. Click on **Code Downloads & Errata**.
4. Enter the name of the book in the **Search** box and follow the onscreen instructions.

Once the file is downloaded, please make sure that you unzip or extract the folder using the latest version of:

- WinRAR/7-Zip for Windows
- Zipeg/iZip/UnRarX for Mac
- 7-Zip/PeaZip for Linux

The code bundle for the book is also hosted on GitHub at https://github.com/PacktPublishing/Server-Side-Development-with-Node.js-and-Koa.js-Quick-Start-Guide. In case there's an update to the code, it will be updated on the existing GitHub repository.

We also have other code bundles from our rich catalog of books and videos available at https://github.com/PacktPublishing/. Check them out!

Download the color images

We also provide a PDF file that has color images of the screenshots/diagrams used in this book. You can download it here: `https://www.packtpub.com/sites/default/files/downloads/9781789345391_ColorImages.pdf`.

Code in action

Visit the following link to check out videos of the code being run:
`http://bit.ly/2P9N0Fx`

Conventions used

There are a number of text conventions used throughout this book.

`CodeInText`: Indicates code words in text, database table names, folder names, filenames, file extensions, pathnames, dummy URLs, user input, and Twitter handles. Here is an example: "Mount the downloaded `WebStorm-10*.dmg` disk image file as another disk in your system."

A block of code is set as follows:

```
function logTimeUp() {
   console.log("Time up!");
}
setTimeout(logTimeUp, 1000);
```

When we wish to draw your attention to a particular part of a code block, the relevant lines or items are set in bold:

```
dataPromise()
   .then(data => console.log(`Here is ${data}`));

// Here is some important data!
```

Any command-line input or output is written as follows:

```
npm install Koa
```

Bold: Indicates a new term, an important word, or words that you see on screen. For example, words in menus or dialog boxes appear in the text like this. Here is an example: "Select **System info** from the **Administration** panel."

Warnings or important notes appear like this.

 Tips and tricks appear like this.

Get in touch

Feedback from our readers is always welcome.

General feedback: If you have questions about any aspect of this book, mention the book title in the subject of your message and email us at `customercare@packtpub.com`.

Errata: Although we have taken every care to ensure the accuracy of our content, mistakes do happen. If you have found a mistake in this book, we would be grateful if you would report this to us. Please visit `www.packt.com/submit-errata`, selecting your book, clicking on the Errata Submission Form link, and entering the details.

Piracy: If you come across any illegal copies of our works in any form on the internet, we would be grateful if you would provide us with the location address or website name. Please contact us at `copyright@packt.com` with a link to the material.

If you are interested in becoming an author: If there is a topic that you have expertise in, and you are interested in either writing or contributing to a book, please visit `authors.packtpub.com`.

Reviews

Please leave a review. Once you have read and used this book, why not leave a review on the site that you purchased it from? Potential readers can then see and use your unbiased opinion to make purchase decisions, we at Packt can understand what you think about our products, and our authors can see your feedback on their book. Thank you!

For more information about Packt, please visit `packt.com`.

1
Introducing Koa

Node.js, which was introduced in 2009, has become very popular for building applications and APIs on the web. One of the major factors that influenced its increase in popularity is the fact that developers can now use a single language for developing their applications, both on the server side and client side. JavaScript developers who usually only worked on client-side applications in the past could now work on server-side applications with the same development stack. This increase in popularity and adoption has led to a lot of community enthusiasm and support, which by extension has caused a lot of frameworks and plugins being developed to optimize scripting and software development in Node.js.

Many of these frameworks are focused on different ideologies and functionalities. Express.js, with over four million weekly downloads as at the time of writing, is one of the more popular frameworks for Node.js. It was built to be a very simple and unopinionated framework for quickly building out web applications in Node.js. Koa.js was built to be an improvement on Express.js, with the same underlying philosophy.

Since its introduction, JavaScript has continually evolved and every iteration brings with it advantages and upgrades. Koa leverages on a lot of new and shiny things in the newer JavaScript versions, such as the `async... await` syntax. These features are part of what makes Koa a fast and easy-to-use web development tool.

The topics that will be covered in this chapter are the following:

- What is Koa?
- What can you do with Koa?
- Why choose Koa?
- When you should not use Koa
- Introducing Koa2
- Koa versus Express
- How can this book help you understand Koa better?

Technical requirements

To follow along with this chapter, you need the following installed locally:
Node.js (>= v7.6.0) and NPM: You can find download and installation instructions for this on the Node.js official website (`https://nodejs.org/en/`).

If you use macOS, you can make use of the Homebrew package manager to install Node.js easily.

The code files of this chapter can be found on GitHub:
`https://github.com/PacktPublishing/Server-Side-development-with-Node.js-and-Koa.js-Quick-Start-Guide/tree/master/Chapter01`

Check out the following video to see the code in action:
`http://bit.ly/2BH8gz0`

What is Koa?

Koa is a newly popular `Node.js` framework created by the team at Express. It was built to be a more expressive, minimalist, and modern version of its predecessor. As a matter of fact, because of its embrace of modern development techniques in JavaScript, it has been referred to by some people as Express 5.0 in spirit.

Development on the Koa framework started sometime in late 2013 by the same team behind Express. It was decided that adding too many breaking changes to Express would be undesirable; hence, the team decided to take the new ideas it had to create a new framework, while development continued on Express itself in parallel. Koa was initially written to leverage the `async` goodness of the then-newly introduced JavaScript generators. Since then, Koa has been rewritten using the more modern `async...await`, making the code base even cleaner.

With around 2K **LOC (lines of code)**, Koa can boast a very minimalistic code footprint. Koa is also very unopinionated; in fact, it does not ship with any middleware out of the box. Instead, it leaves these decisions to the developers. Developers can choose to either build out the middleware they need or take advantage of the ones built by other developers that are publicly available online.

By making use of the modern JavaScript `async... await` syntax, Koa allows developers to escape *callback hell* and handle errors better. Its futuristic approach to development in JavaScript makes it a choice for developers who enjoy trying out new things. If you are unfamiliar with what `async... await` is, not to worry, we will be covering it in following chapters.

What can you do with Koa?

So, you have heard about Koa, and are trying to decide whether you should get into it. What could be the deciding factor is the use case you have in mind. After all, in the world of software development tools and frameworks, what really matters is what you are capable of doing with these tools and frameworks.

If you want to build scalable web applications and APIs in JavaScript, then Koa is a good fit. Koa can be used to create a range of web applications such as forums, e-commerce websites, and social networks. You can use Koa to build something as simple as a to-do list application or something as complicated as an e-commerce website.

Koa is also great for building services such as **Representational State Transfer (REST)** APIs that could provide data to be used by frontend applications. REST APIs that are built in Koa are a good choice for frontend applications written in plain JavaScript, Angular, React, Vue.js, or any other **User Interface (UI)** framework.

Why choose Koa?

At this point, you may be thinking, "*Why exactly should I use Koa, amid the myriad of Node.js frameworks available? What exactly makes Koa special or different?*" That would be an excellent question. We will cover the answer to that in this section and list some reasons why Koa is a great choice for your next web development project.

As mentioned earlier, Koa is highly unopinionated, which makes its capabilities limited only by the developer's imagination. It is a framework that provides a light and highly configurable base for developers to quickly get started building out their web applications in JavaScript. Some of the things that make Koa a great choice include the following:

- **Embraces modern standards**: Koa embraces the more modern JavaScript ES6 syntax and encourages its use. The more modern syntax brings with it some advantages as the language evolves with every iteration.

- **Very light**: Koa is one of the lightest frameworks out there with around 2K LOC. It only comes with the bare minimum. This shows developers that the framework is simply there to help do the bare minimum needed for them to quickly develop their apps and not more or less.
- **Highly unopinionated**: Koa tries as much as possible not to restrict developers. It does not come with any middleware out of the box, not even for routing. Koa's aim is to allow developers to be even more expressive. Koa encourages developers to either develop any middleware they need or take advantage of the publicly available ones. The Koa core team has developed a number of middlewares that are available for developers to plug into their application if so needed.
- **Ease of creating custom middleware**: Middleware functions are functions that sit between requests and responses in an application. They can usually manipulate both the request and responses in an application. A key factor in middleware function definition is also calling the next middleware to be executed. Koa's middleware cascading pattern is also one of the reasons Koa is recommended. The cascading pattern makes implementing and understanding the flow of middleware in your applications very easy. Simple middleware in Koa can be defined and registered in as few as three lines, as seen in the following code snippet:

```
app.use(async (context, next) => {
    console.log(`Time: ${Date.now()}`);
    await next();
});
```

This code snippet is simple middleware for logging the time when a request is made to the server in Koa.

- **Community support**: As a result of its increase in popularity, a lot of plugins and middleware have been built and made publicly available. There are also a lot of JavaScript developers available to help answer questions and discuss issues related to the framework on popular forums.

- **Ease to get started with**: One of the things JavaScript developers who are familiar with Express love about the framework is how easy it is to get started with it. Koa also embraces that simplicity and makes it very easy for developers to get started with it. Little configuration has to be done to cascade a simple Koa application. To illustrate how easy it is to get started with Koa, here is a Koa `Hello World` app, as seen on the Koa official website:

```
// ./server.js

const Koa = require('koa');
const app = new Koa();

app.use(asyncctx => {
  ctx.body = 'Hello World';
});

app.listen(3000);
```

- **Flexible**: Koa does not enforce folder and file structure; hence, developers can use their preferred file structures when developing applications in Koa.
- **Ease of error handling**: Koa's embrace of the `async... await` JavaScript ES6 syntax makes error handling much easier. It is also easy to define middleware in Koa to handle errors thrown at different points in your application.
- **Database and ORM agnostic**: Developers can create web applications that will use their database and **Object Relation Mapper (ORM)** of choice. They are not forced to stick to a particular database or ORM as defined by the framework. Databases such as `MySQL`, `MongoDB`, and `PostgreSQL` can be used with Koa. ORMs such as `Mongoose`, `Sequelize`,and `Knex` are also easy to integrate with the Koa framework.
- **The similarity to Express**: If you are like many Node developers, you have at one point or the other worked with Express. This familiarity with Express proves to be an asset when working with Koa, as it makes it easier to get accustomed to Koa and its philosophy. This also works the other way around too. If you get familiar with Koa before Express, it becomes easier for you to pick up Express projects and understand them.
- **Concise code**: Writing code in Koa is generally more concise than in other `Node.js` frameworks. This is because it ditches the use of callbacks and encourages the modern ES6 syntax. It also has a number of HTTP utilities bundled with it to make writing web applications an easier experience.

- **Escape callback hell**: As a result of Koa's reliance on modern standards in JavaScript development, we are able to avoid dealing with nested callbacks and the phenomenon known as **callback hell** when developing our applications. To illustrate this, here is an example of how an endpoint to retrieve all of the products in a category from a database would look in Express with the use of callbacks:

```
// ./express-route.js

app.get('/category/:slug', (req, res, next)) => {
  const { slug } = req.params;

  Category.findOne({ slug }, (err, category) => {
    if (err) {
      return next(err);
    }

    Product.find({ category: category.id }, (err, products)
      => {
      if (err) {
        return next(err);
      }

      res.send(products);
    });
  });
});
```

The same endpoint can be written in Koa, as seen in the following code snippet:

```
// ./koa-route.js

app.get('/category/:slug', async ctx => {
  const { slug } = ctx.params;
  const category = await Category.findOne({ slug });
  const products = await Product.find({ category: category.id });
  ctx.body = products;
});
```

From these examples, we can see clearly how much more readable the code written in Koa is. We can avoid nested callbacks with the use of promises and the `async... await` syntax.

When you should not use Koa

Although Koa is a great choice for building HTTP services and web applications, it is not always the best option for all projects. Just like with every framework, language, and even design pattern, the very things that are advantages become drawbacks when dealing with certain use cases. It is best to judge the use of Koa on a case by case basis and make use of it only when it is a good fit for the particular project.

Generally, Koa will not be a great choice for you if you are not willing to try out the newer JavaScript ES6 syntax. Koa was built for the modern web. If, for some reason, your project has a strict requirement to use an older version of JavaScript, Koa would not be suitable.

If you would also prefer a framework with a lot of boilerplate code and a defined structure, you might have to look at other frameworks such as `hapi.js` and `AdonisJs`. Koa, much like Express, prides itself on minimalism and allowing developers to be expressive. Having a lot of boilerplate and a strict code structure are not philosophies Koa embraces.

It is also important to note that Koa is a framework built on top of JavaScript and `Node.js`. As Koa inherits the advantages of Node, such as being fast at performing network and asynchronous operations, it also inherits some of the drawbacks and limitations that are present in Node. Koa would not be an ideal choice for a project where JavaScript is not the language of choice.

Koa versus Express

Koa and Express share a lot of similarities, as the development of the two frameworks was kickstarted by the same team. While a lot of the underlying philosophies between Koa and Express are the same, clear differences exist as the creators of the frameworks attempted to do things in a different way with the release of Koa.

A major difference is in the philosophy of the two frameworks. Whereas Express complements Node, Koa attempts to fix and replace many things in it. The major difference is the fact that Koa tries to completely ditch callbacks and avoid callback hell by making use of `promises` and `async` functions.

Unlike Express, which augments Node's request (`req`) and response (`res`) objects with additional parameters and methods, Koa provides its own `ctx.request` and `ctx.response` objects. According to the Koa documentation, the following is true:

> *"Koa can be viewed as an abstraction of Node.js's* `http` *modules, whereas Express is an application framework for Node.js."*

Koa tries to fix some of the things wrong with Node and provides a simple, lightweight, and unopinionated framework for building out HTTP services.

Some other differences between Koa and Express include the following:

- **Router**: Koa does not include a router out of the box; instead, external middleware is available to be used as routers such as `koa-router` and `koa-route`. Express, on the other hand, comes bundled with a router out of the box.

- **Templating**: Express has support for various popular templating engines out of the box, including `Jade`, `Pug`, `EJS`,and `Mustache`. In contrast, Koa requires installing an external plugin/middleware to support templating engines. A popular plugin for templating in Koa is `koa-views`.

- **Convenience utilities**: Express includes some convenience utilities (`https://expressjs.com/en/resources/utils.html`) to help programmers handle regular tasks such as file streaming and URL parsing. Koa does not include these utilities.

- **Promise-based control flow**: Koa has the advantage of ditching callbacks and avoiding callback hell by making heavy use of promises, unlike its predecessor, Express. This ensures that errors are easier to handle without many `try...catch` statements.

- **Cascading middleware pattern of flow in Koa.js**: This allows middleware to take action exactly twice for each request whereas express middleware allows for only single execution per request. This flexibility allows Koa middleware developers to use the patterns established in other languages and systems such as `Ruby's Rack`.

Here is a table from the Koa documentation, comparing it to Express:

Feature	Koa	Express
Middleware Kernel	✓	✓
Routing		✓
Templating		✓
Sending files		✓
JSONP		✓

How can this book help you understand Koa better?

This book takes a practical approach to teach JavaScript developers how to understand the Koa framework. In the course of this book, we will examine important concepts in Koa, such as the request, response, and context objects. We will also look at other concepts that will be helpful for building real-world applications such as request and error handling.

We will build two applications to reinforce the concepts we learned about Koa. These applications will include a REST API and a fully-fledged web application.

As we build the REST API, we will learn how to create routes, handle requests, and send responses from their APIs. We will also learn practically how the context object works for API creation. We will build an API that will have **CRUD (Create, Read, Update,** and **Delete)** functionality; hence, we will also be interacting with a database. Building a real-life application will also afford us the chance to learn about how you can decide to structure your Koa applications.

Building the fully-fledged web application will allow us to learn how to build an application in Koa with views and templates. We will also learn how to authenticate, handle forms, handle sessions, and so on, in the framework.

Summary

In this chapter, we introduced Koa and talked about its benefits for server-side web development. We talked about what developers can build with Koa and established some of its many advantages. We were also able to talk about cases when using Koa might not be ideal.

Finally, we talked about how this book is structured and how it will help you learn and understand the Koa framework better.

The next chapter will cover getting started with Koa. In the next chapter, we will learn how to get started with server-side development with Koa. We will learn how to install Koa, create a simple server, and build the obligatory `Hello World` app. The chapter will introduce us to some hands-on work in Koa, and we will begin to explore why Koa is so highly recommended.

2
Getting Started with Koa

One of the things that makes Koa so desirable to work with is the ease of getting started with it. Taking after Express, all of the logic for a simple web application can be contained in a single JavaScript file with Koa. This works to our benefit and is especially great if you are just willing to test the framework out before taking a deep dive.

In this chapter, we are going to get our hands dirty and get into the code. We will be exploring the basic concepts of Koa and will build our first server-side application in Koa.

Some of the topics we will cover in this chapter include the following:

- Modern JavaScript
- A primer on Node
- What is `async... await`?
- Using Babel
- Installing Koa
- Starting a server in Koa

Technical requirements

To follow along with this chapter, you need the following installed locally:

- **Node.js (>= v7.6.0) and NPM:** You can find download and installation instructions for this on the Node.js official website (`https://nodejs.org/en/`).

If you use macOS, you can make use of the Homebrew package manager to install Node.js and MongoDB easily.

The code files of this chapter can be found on GitHub:
`https://github.com/PacktPublishing/Server-Side-development-with-Node.js-and-Koa.js-Quick-Start-Guide/tree/master/Chapter02`

Check out the following video to see the code in action:
`http://bit.ly/2Q2gRoV`

Modern JavaScript

Before we get into `Node.js` and writing code in Koa, we should take a quick look at the modern JavaScript ES6, ES7 (and beyond) syntaxes and the advantages they bring. ES6 (or ES 2015) and ES7 (or ES 2016) are major updates to the JavaScript language that brought a lot of new features and optimized the language for readability and simplicity.

Some of the key features introduced by ES6 include `let`, `const`, object destructuring, the spread operator, and so on. The `async... await` syntax, which is heavily used by Koa, is a new feature introduced in ES7. Some other key features introduced by ES7 are destructuring assignment (`https://developer.mozilla.org/en-US/docs/Web/JavaScript/Reference/Operators/Destructuring_assignment`) and Observables (`https://developer.mozilla.org/en-US/docs/Web/JavaScript/Reference/Global_Objects/Object/observe`). Beyond ES6 and Es7, a lot of new features are continually being implemented in JavaScript. Embracing these new features helps to keep up with the best practices and constantly improve the quality of the code we write.

The introduction of modern syntaxes and functions have made it possible for JavaScript developers to write concise and maintainable code, without the need to sacrifice performance. On the contrary, a lot of the new features make it possible to do more things in the language. Some of these things were done in the past using external libraries that exposed helper functions. Examples of such libraries include `Lodash` and `Underscore.js`.

 Most code examples in this book use the newer ES6/ES7 JavaScript features. Ensure you have a recent version of JavaScript running on your machine so as to be able to follow along adequately.

A primer on Node

As JavaScript developers who may or may not have experience working with Node.js, a brief introduction to Node.js and its core ideology will help get everyone up to speed. Node.js, or simply Node, is a run-time environment that executes JavaScript outside a browser. In simpler terms, and as it relates to web developers, Node is a platform that allows developers to write JavaScript applications that can also act as servers.

JavaScript became popular for being a language used to manipulate the **DOM (Document Object Model)** on web pages. It was a language typically used for client-side scripting. Node, which was built on Chrome's open source v8 JavaScript engine, made it possible to run JavaScript both on the browser and the server. This was highly accepted, as developers could now develop applications with the same language on servers and web browsers.

Node is very fast and is a great choice for building HTTP applications. It processes incoming requests in a loop, called the **event loop**, which allows the development of fast web servers in JavaScript. Its event-driven architecture allows asynchronous operations. This means that developers can create highly scalable applications capable of processing requests asynchronously without using threading.

Asynchronous programming in Node is one of the reasons the language is so widely adopted. If you are unfamiliar with asynchronous programming or its benefits and how it compares to synchronous programming, here is a good example of a program that needs to make a request to get data from two external sources:

- **In a synchronous program**: The logical thing to do would be to make a request to the first external source, get a response, and then make another request to the second external source and merge the results. While this is a flow that is logical and easy to follow, it means that the wait time to service another request will be at least the sum of the wait times for each individual request. Since synchronous code leads to resource and event blocking, it does not lead an efficient solution and effectively slows down our application due to poor resource utilization.
- **In an asynchronous program**: Both requests can be made in parallel. When each request is completed, it notifies the main program and the results can be combined after the request that took the longest is completed. In this case, the wait time is only the time it takes for the slower request to be completed. Also, neither of the requests cause resource/event blocking, which would allow our program to respond to more new requests while waiting for results for the initial task.

Managing asynchronous actions can get quite complicated, especially in programs where the flow of logic should be synchronous. Callback functions can be used to manage asynchronous operations. Callback functions are functions that are passed to another function (the main function) to be executed inside the main function. Here's a simple example of using a callback function with the `setTimeout()` function:

```
function logTimeUp() {
   console.log("Time up!");
}

setTimeout(logTimeUp, 1000);
```

The `setTimeout` function in JavaScript waits a given number of milliseconds and then executes the callback function passed to it. In the previous code example, we define a callback function called `logTimeUp` that simply prints `Time up!` to `stdout`. We then pass this function as a parameter to the `setTimeout` function, which will execute the callback function after `1000` milliseconds (one second). This is a classic example of how callbacks work.

In modern JavaScript, asynchronous actions can be modeled using `Promises`, which can be managed and consumed in multiple ways. One of these ways is using the `async... await` syntax.

What is async... await?

Asynchronous functions are functions that work asynchronously. They return a `Promise` class implicitly and can run concurrently. We will be discussing two major ways to define asynchronous functions. These include the following:

- Using the native `Promise` class
- Using the modern `Async` keyword

The `await` keyword is used inside an asynchronous function to resolve a promise. Async and await are usually used together for managing the control of flow in a modern asynchronous JavaScript application. Koa relies heavily on `async.. await` to avoid callback hell and provide a more convenient method for handling errors.

The promise class

Before introducing `async`, let's discuss a little about the native `Promise` class in JavaScript. As mentioned, promises are the way modern JavaScript manages asynchronous actions. The standard `Promise` class can be used for creating promises. A promise can be defined as seen in the following code snippet:

```
const dataPromise = new Promise((resolve, reject) => resolve("some
important data!"));
```

From the preceding code block, we can see that a function is passed to the `Promise` constructor—this function is called an `executor` function. This executor has two arguments passed into it, which are used to determine two important properties of the resulting promise—its `state` and `result` properties.

The default value of `state` is `pending`, which then changes to either `fulfilled` or `rejected`. The default value of `result` is `undefined`, which then changes to any value of your choosing.

The two functions an executor receives as arguments are `resolve(value)` and `reject(error)`. The `resolve(value)` function indicates that the promise was successfully completed, and hence it sets the `state` of the promise to `fulfilled` and assigns `value` to its `result` property. The reject function indicates that a promise failed (an error occurred) and accordingly sets the `state` propertyof the promise to `rejected` and assigns `error` to its `result` property.

The result of the promise defined previously can be obtained using its `.then()` function, as seen here:

```
dataPromise()
  .then(data => console.log(`Here is ${data}`));

// Here is some important data!
```

In the case of failures, promises can also be rejected in a like manner. Here's a promise definition that throws an error or rejection:

```
const dataPromise = new Promise((resolve, reject) => reject(new Error('data
failure!')));
```

When retrieving results for the previous promise, the error can be handled with the `.catch()` function:

```
dataPromise()
  .catch(error => console.log(`Data retrieval failed. ${error}`));

// Data retrieval failed. Error: data failure!
```

Introducing async

Another way to create and resolve promises is to use the `async... await` syntax. Async is basically syntactical sugar around the `Promise` class. The `dataPromise` promise we defined earlier with the `Promise` class can be defined with `async` as follows:

```
async dataPromise() {
  return "some important data!";
}
```

Rejections can also be defined simply by throwing errors within the `async` function:

```
async dataPromise() {
  throw new Error('data failure');
}
```

Introducing await

The `await` keyword helps us manage promises in a more procedural manner. The `await` keyword can be only used inside an `async` (asynchronous) function to resolve a promise. It helps us resolve promises just like the `.then()` function we saw earlier. `Async... await` is the cleanest way to control the flow of a modern asynchronous JavaScript application. An example can be seen here:

```
async function getPostCategory() {
  const postId = 123;
  const post = await Post.findById(postId);
  return post.category;
}
```

The preceding code block is essentially the same as the one shown here, using the `.then()` function:

```
function getPostCategory() {
  const postId = 123;

  return Post.findById(postId).then(post => {
    return post.category;
  });
}
```

Note: The `await` keyword can only be used in `async` functions.

As seen in the preceding code examples, using `async` and `await`, we are able to clearly follow the flow of data in an asynchronous application. Koa takes advantage of this, hence making middleware definition and error handling much easier.

Installing Koa

To install Koa, you need to have the following installed locally:

- **Node (preferably > 7.6)**: This can be obtained from the Node homepage (`https://nodejs.org/en`).
- **NPM**: This is the official package manager for JavaScript and is usually installed along with the Node installation.

With Node and NPM installed, you only need to run this command on your Terminal to install Koa to your application:

```
npm install Koa
```

Note: If you are using an npm of 5 and above, you do not need to use the `--save` flag to save installs as dependencies in your `package.json`. If you are using a lesser version, you will need to add the flag. You can also simply run `npm i koa` to install Koa and save it as a dependency in newer versions of npm.

Using Babel

If you're using an older version of Node (< 7.6), you will need to use a transpiler such as Babel to make `async` functions compatible with your version of Node. Koa recommends using Babel's require hook, as seen in the example in the following code snippet (`https://babeljs.io/docs/en/babel-register/`):

```
require('babel-register');

// require the rest of the app that needs to be transpiled after the hook

const app = require('./app');
```

You can then install the transforms you would need, depending on your version of Node. If you are using V6 of Node, you would not need most of the transforms, since it already supports a lot of ES6 features. At the minimum though, you would need the `transform-async-to-generator` plugin. You can define this in your `.babelrc` file, as follows:

```
{
   "plugins": ["transform-async-to-generator"]
}
```

According to the Koa documentation, you can also use the `env` preset with a target option `"node": "current"` instead.

Starting a server in Koa

To get started with starting a server in Koa, we should first create a project directory and enter that directory. We can do so with the following commands:

```
mkdir koa-server
cd koa-server
```

Next, we initialize a project in `npm` with the following command:

```
npm init
```

After running this command, follow the prompts to help create a `package.json` file for your project.

You can run `npm init -y` to create a `package.json` file for your project with default values.

Next, we can install Koa to our project with the following command:

```
npm i koa
```

Now that we have Koa installed, we can create our server file. Let's call the file `index.js`. If you are using a Unix-based operating system such as Linux or macOS, you can create the file with the following command:

```
touch index.js
```

This file will serve as the entry point to our application, and we will write the main logic for our simple server in this file. Using your code or text editor of choice, write the following into the `index.js` file:

```
// ./index.js

const Koa = require('koa');
const app = new Koa();

app.use(async ctx => {
  ctx.body = 'Hello World';
});

app.listen(1234, () => {
  console.log('Server is running on port 1234')
});
```

In the preceding code snippet, first, we require the needed Koa application class and assign it to the `Koa` variable. Next, we initialize a new Koa application instance with `new Koa()` and assign it to `app`. One interesting thing we see next is the definition of a simple middleware.

The middleware we define simply sends back the text `Hello World` as a response to every request. We define the middleware using the `.use()` method available in Koa. The `.use()` method accepts the middleware function as its only argument. The middleware function also takes the context object (defined as `ctx`) as its only argument, which it uses to process requests and send responses. It specifically uses the `context.body` method to send the `Hello World` response. If you feel a little lost at this point, don't worry. We will discuss more Koa core concepts and the context object in `Chapter 3`, *Koa Core Concepts*.

Finally, we start the server with the `app.listen()` function, which takes the port to run the server as its first argument. In our case, we defined `1234` as the port to run our server on. The second argument is a callback function, which is called once the server starts.

We can now start the app with the following command:

```
node index.js
```

This starts our server, and if we visit `http://localhost:1234`, we will see the `Hello World` response. We can also test this in the Terminal using the `curl` command:

```
curl -i http://localhost:1234
```

It should send back a response similar to this:

```
HTTP/1.1 200 OK
Content-Type: text/plain; charset=utf-8
Content-Length: 11
Connection: keep-alive
Hello World
```

Summary

In this chapter, we learned about Node and how asynchrony in JavaScript works. We also learned about the different ways asynchronous actions in JavaScript are handled, including the `async... await` syntax.

After the primer, we dug into writing some code and started a very light server in Koa. This showed us the prerequisites of Koa, how to install the framework, and how to get started on it.

In the next chapter, we will learn about the core concepts of Koa. We will learn about the application, context, request, and response objects in Koa. We will also learn how to create and use middleware. We will go into details about Koa's philosophy and show readers how the different parts of the framework work.

3
Koa Core Concepts

In this chapter, we will learn about core concepts in Koa, including the application and context objects. We will also dig further into the context object that houses the request and response objects. We will see how Koa provides methods around its request and response facilities.

The concept of middlewares in Koa will also be properly discussed in this chapter. We will introduce and explain middleware definition and functionality in Koa. We will use code examples to show clearly how the flow of logic with middleware works in Koa.

The topics we will cover in the chapter include the following:

- The application object
- The context object
- The request object
- The response object
- Middleware

Technical requirements

You need the following installed locally:

- **Node.js (>= v7.6.0) and NPM**: You can find download and installation instructions for this on the Node.js official website (https://nodejs.org/en/).
- **MongoDB**: This is one of the most popular NoSQL databases in the world. It is open source, and you can find download instructions on its official website (https://www.mongodb.com/) as well.

If you use macOS, you can make use of the Homebrew package manager to install Node.js and MongoDB easily.

The code files of this chapter can be found on GitHub:
`https://github.com/PacktPublishing/Server-Side-development-with-Node.js-and-`
`Koa.js-Quick-Start-Guide/tree/master/Chapter03`

Check out the following video to see the code in action:
`http://bit.ly/2QssJ2J`

The application object

The application object in Koa is an object containing the Koa application instance. It also contains a list of the middleware functions in the application. It is responsible for managing and executing the middleware in a cascaded manner. It is also responsible for managing some key aspects of the application, as we will soon see in some of the following examples. Here is an excerpt from the Koa official documentation:

> *"A Koa application is an object containing an array of middleware functions which are composed and executed in a stack-like manner upon request. Koa is similar to many other middleware systems that you may have encountered such as Ruby's Rack, Connect, and so on—however, a key design decision was made to provide high level sugar at the otherwise low-level middleware layer. This improves interoperability, robustness, and makes writing middleware much more enjoyable."*

The application object also exposes methods for common tasks such as content-negotiation, cache freshness, proxy support, and so on. A useless Koa application that runs on port 1234 can be easily created in just a few lines of code, as shown here:

```
const Koa = require('koa');
const app = new Koa();

const port = 1234;
app.listen(port, () => {
  console.log(`The app is running on port ${port}`);
});
```

In the preceding application, the application object is referenced by the app variable by instantiating the application with `new Koa()`. We then use the application object to start the server with `app.listen()`, one of the various methods exposed on the application object.

Useful application methods

As mentioned earlier, the application object exposes some methods to make development easier and make some tasks easier to do. In this section, we will discuss some of the methods available in the application method:

- `app.listen(...)`: The `app.listen()` method is used to create and return an HTTP Server. It is syntactical sugar around the native Node `server.listen()` method. It can be used as seen here:

  ```
  const Koa = require('koa');
  const app = new Koa();
  app.listen(3000);
  ```

The preceding code block is essentially the same as the following one:

```
const http = require('http');
const Koa = require('koa');
const app = new Koa();
http.createServer(app.callback()).listen(3000);
```

One or more Koa applications can be mounted on the same HTTP server, as creating a Koa application does not directly map to starting a server. Here is an example where a single Koa application is started as HTTP and HTTPS on two different ports:

```
const http = require('http');
const https = require('https');
const Koa = require('koa');
const app = new Koa();
http.createServer(app.callback()).listen(3000);
https.createServer(app.callback()).listen(3001);
```

- `app.callback()`: The `app.callback()` method returns a callback function to be used by the `http.createServer()` method for handling a request. Its usage can be seen in the preceding examples, when we start a simple Koa app with the `http.createServer()` or `https.createServer()` methods.

- `app.use(function)`: This is used for registering middleware to the application. It is similar to the `app.use()` method implemented in Express. It takes the middleware function as its only argument.

A simple middleware for logging the time a request is made can be defined with `app.use()` as seen here:

```
app.use(async ctx => {
   const currentDateTime = new Date().toLocaleString();
   console.log(`${ctx.method} request made to ${ctx.url} at
${currentDateTime}`;
   await next();
});
```

- `app.keys=`: This is used to set signed cookie keys. The keys are passed to `KeyGrip`, and can be set in the following ways:

  ```
  app.keys = ['first secret key', 'second secret key']; // passing
  an array of keys
  ```

  ```
  app.keys = new KeyGrip(['first secret key', 'second secret key'],
  'sha256'); // passing KeyGrip instance
  ```

Keygrip is a library for signing and verifying data through a rotating credential system in Node.js. With KeyGrip, new server keys can be added and old ones removed regularly, without invalidating the client credentials.

Passing the KeyGrip instance as opposed to passing in an array of keys to `app.keys=` gives you the flexibility to set other options such as the `hmacAlgorithm` and `encoding` for your signed keys. The documentation for KeyGrip and what these options mean can be found here: `https://www.npmjs.com/package/keygrip`.

The keys may be rotated and are used when signing cookies with the `signed: true` option:

```
context.cookies.set('color', 'red', { signed: true });
```

- `app.context`: This is the prototype from which the context object (usually referred to as `ctx`) is created. It can be used to append more methods to the context object, so as to make them available throughout your application. This can be seen in this example, where a logger is attached:

  ```
  app.context.logger = logger();

  app.use(async ctx => {
     ctx.logger.info('Accessing middleware...')
  });
  ```

Settings

The application settings are properties set on the application instance. The following are currently supported:

- `app.env`: This defaults to the `NODE_ENV` or `development`.
- `app.proxy`: When set to `true`, proxy header fields will be trusted. This simply means that the `X-Forwarded-*` header fields may be trusted.
- `app.subdomainOffset` offset of `.subdomains` to ignore. Its value is 2 by default. The use of this can be illustrated with an example taken from the Koa documentation:

  > *"...if the domain is* `"tobi.ferrets.example.com"`*: If* `app.subdomainOffset` *is not set,* `ctx.subdomains` *is* `["ferrets", "tobi"]`*. If* `app.subdomainOffset` *is 3,* `ctx.subdomains` *is* `["tobi"]`*."*

The context object

The Koa context object usually referred to as `ctx` is a combination of Node's request and response objects into a single object. A new context is created per request. It can be accessed in a middleware function as the first argument in the function.

It is often referenced in middleware as the `ctx` identifier, as seen in the following example:

```
app.use(async ctx => {
  ctx; // context object
  ctx.request; // Request object
  ctx.response; // Response object
});
```

The context object contains methods and properties which either belong specifically to the object or are aliases of methods and properties in the request and response objects.

Both the request and response objects will be discussed in detail in later sections

Context object API

The context object exposes various methods and properties to help with HTTP application development and middleware creation. In this way, Koa varies from its predecessor, Express, in that the many functions needed for development can be accessed simply via the context object instead of needing to access the request (`req`) and response (`res`) objects separately.

Some of the methods and properties exposed on the Context object include the following:

- `ctx.req`: This serves as a reference to the request object in Node. Note that this differs from the Koa request object.

For example, you can access an object containing the request headers by using the `req.headers` property, as seen here:

```
console.log(ctx.req.headers);

// => { host: 'localhost:1234',
//   'user-agent': 'curl/7.54.0',
//   accept: '*/*' }
```

- `ctx.res`: Similar to `ctx.req`, this serves as a reference to the response object in Node. Note that bypassing Koa's response handling is not supported by Koa currently. Hence, Node response methods that directly attempt to write or manipulate the response body should be avoided, such as the following:
  - `res.statusCode`
  - `res.writeHead()`
  - `res.write()`
  - `res.end()`

The `ctx.res` object can be used in the following manner:

```
ctx.res.setHeader('Content-Type', 'text/html');

console.log(ctx.res.getHeader('Content-Type'));
// => text/html
```

- `ctx.request`: This is an instance of the Koa request object. It provides access to all the request related methods and properties needed for HTTP application development. This object will be discussed in further details in later sections.

The request object can be used, for example, to retrieve the origin of a request, as seen in the example here:

```
console.log(ctx.request.origin);

// => http://localhost:1234
```

- `ctx.response`: This is an instance of the Koa response object. Similar to the Koa request object, it provides everyday functionality for building out HTTP applications. It will also be discussed in more detail in later sections of this chapter.

Here is an example of how you can use the response object to set the HTTP status for a response in Koa:

```
ctx.response.status = 200;

console.log(ctx.response.message);
// => Ok
```

- `ctx.state`: This is the namespace recommend by Koa for passing data throughout your application. A good use case of this is passing some data across middleware and to your views, as seen in this example:

```
// middleware for retrieving user details
app.use(async ctx => {
  ctx.state.user = await User.find(id);
});

// middleware to send response back to user
app.use(async ctx => {
  const { user } = ctx.state;
  ctx.body = `Hello, ${user.name}`;
});
```

- `ctx.app`: This is a reference to the Koa application instance discussed earlier in this chapter. This reference allows us to make use of the application object in our middleware. For example, this is a middleware we can use to log information depending on the environment our application is running in:

```
app.use(async (ctx, next) => {
  const { env } = ctx.app;
  if (env === 'development') {
    console.log(`request made to ${ctx.request.url}`);
  }
  await next();
});
```

- `ctx.cookies`: This object consists of two methods for interacting with cookies. Koa uses the `cookies` module and simply passes the options. The two methods available for use are:
  - `ctx.cookies.get(name, [options])`: This returns the value of a cookie named `name` with `options`.
  - `ctx.cookies.set(name, [options])`: This sets cookie `name` with `options`.

These methods can be used in the following manner:

```
ctx.cookies.set('SESSION_ID', '1234');

// after response has been sent and the
// cookie has been set on the client
console.log(ctx.cookies.get('SESSION_ID'));
// => 1234
```

- `ctx.throw([status], [msg], [properties])`: This is a helper method that throws an HTTP error with a status as a response. This makes use of the `http-errors` module. Here are some simple example usages of the method:

```
ctx.throw(401);
ctx.throw(401, 'Unauthorized');
ctx.throw(401, 'Unathourized', { user });
```

- `ctx.assert(value, [status], [msg], [properties])`: This is a helper method that throws an error similar to the `ctx.throw` method when value is a `false value`. Koa makes use of `http-assert` for assertions.

- `ctx.respond`: Koa's default response handling can be turned off by explicitly setting `ctx.respond` to `false`. This can be used if a decision is made to manually write to the `res` object, instead of utilizing Koa's response handling. This behavior is currently not supported by Koa and could cause unexpected results.

Aliases

The context object exposes aliases for common-use properties and methods the request and response objects. These are present to make development faster and reduce the amount of code developers need to write.

For example, the `.header` property that exists in the request object can be accessed directly from the context object, as seen in the code block as follows:

```
console.log(ctx.header);

// => { host: 'localhost:1234',
//   'user-agent': 'curl/7.54.0',
//   accept: '*/
```

Similarly, the `.body` setter that exists in the response object can be accessed directly via the context object, as seen in the following code block:

```
ctx.body = 'Hello, World';
```

These are the aliases present for the `Request` object:

- `ctx.header`
- `ctx.headers`
- `ctx.method`
- `ctx.method=`
- `ctx.url`
- `ctx.url=`
- `ctx.originalUrl`
- `ctx.origin`
- `ctx.href`
- `ctx.path`

- `ctx.path=`
- `ctx.query`
- `ctx.query=`
- `ctx.querystring`
- `ctx.querystring=`
- `ctx.host`
- `ctx.hostname`
- `ctx.fresh`
- `ctx.stale`
- `ctx.socket`
- `ctx.protocol`
- `ctx.secure`
- `ctx.ip`
- `ctx.ips`
- `ctx.subdomains`
- `ctx.is()`
- `ctx.accepts()`
- `ctx.acceptsEncodings()`
- `ctx.acceptsCharsets()`
- `ctx.acceptsLanguages()`
- `ctx.get()`

These are the aliases present for the `Response` object:

- `ctx.body`
- `ctx.body=`
- `ctx.status`
- `ctx.status=`
- `ctx.message`
- `ctx.message=`
- `ctx.length=`
- `ctx.length`
- `ctx.type=`

- `ctx.type`
- `ctx.headerSent`
- `ctx.redirect()`
- `ctx.attachment()`
- `ctx.set()`
- `ctx.append()`
- `ctx.remove()`
- `ctx.lastModified=`
- `ctx.etag=`

The request object

The Koa request object is similar to the request object in Node and Express. It can be described as an abstraction of Node's request object. It provides added functionality with its properties and methods for building out everyday HTTP servers.

The methods and properties it exposes include the following:

- `request.header`: This returns an object containing the request headers. This is aliased in the context object, and can also be accessed with `ctx.header`. The following code block shows example usage of how the `request.header` property can be used to retrieve and log the headers from a request:

```
// log the request headers

console.log(ctx.header);
// or
console.log(ctx.request.header);
```

- `request.header=`: This can be used to set the request header object. This can also be accessed with the `ctx.header=` alias. In the following code block, we create a middleware to set the request header before passing control to the next middleware:

```
// set request header
app.use(async (ctx, next) => {
  const header = {
    'accept-encoding': 'gzip'
    // .. other header values
  };
  ctx.request.header = header;
```

```
    await next();
});

// send response back
app.use(async ctx => {
    console.log(ctx.request.header)
    ctx.body = 'Hello World';
});
```

- `request.headers`: This is used to access the request header object. It is an alias of the `request.header` property. It can be used in a similar manner to the `request.header` property as seen here:

```
console.log(ctx.request.headers);

// => { host: 'localhost:1234',
//    'user-agent': 'curl/7.54.0',
//    accept: '*/*' }
```

- `request.headers=`: This is used to set the request header object. It is an alias of the `request.header=` method. It can also be used to set request headers as seen here:

```
ctx.request.headers = {
    'accept-encoding': 'gzip'
};
```

- `request.method`: This is used to access the request method. This is particularly useful for situations where you need to decide on whether to carry out an action based on the HTTP method used. An example can be seen in the code block here:

```
app.use(async ctx => {
    const { method } = ctx.request;
    if (method === 'POST') {
        // carry out validation
    }
});
```

- `request.method=`: This is used to set the request method. A good use case of this is to implement the popular `methodOverrides()` middleware. With this, you can modify request methods to fit what you have defined in your application. This is especially useful when you have a client that only supports simple HTTP verbs such as `GET` and `POST`. Here is an example of its usage:

```
// override request method
app.use(async (ctx, next) => {
        const { method } = ctx.request.query;
    if (method) {
      ctx.request.method = method;
    }
    await next();
});
```

The preceding example code checks whether a custom method type has been passed in the request query string, then overrides the request to fit the desired method.

- `request.length`: This returns the request `Content-Length` as a number, or `undefined` when the `Content-Length` is absent. A request with some data in the request body will show how this property works in the example here:

```
// curl -X POST --data "test data" http://localhost:1234

console.log(ctx.request.length);
// => 9
```

- `request.url`: This returns the request URL.

- `request.url=`: This sets the request URL. The following block can be used for URL rewriting:

```
// url rewrite middleware
app.use(async (ctx, next) => {
  ctx.request.url = '/hello';
  await next();
});
```

- `request.originalUrl`: This returns the request original URL. For a simple app that implements a rewrite to the `/hello` route, a visit to the base `/` route would produce the following results:

```
// rewrite url
app.use(async (ctx, next) => {
  ctx.request.url = '/hello';
  await next();
```

```
  });

  app.use(async ctx => {
    console.log(ctx.request.url);
    // => /hello
    console.log(ctx.request.originalUrl);
    // => /
    ctx.body = 'Hello World';
  });
```

- request.origin: This returns the origin of URL, including the host and protocol. For a local app running on port 1234:

```
console.log(ctx.request.origin);
// => http://localhost:1234
```

- request.href: This returns the full request URL with the protocol, host, and url:

```
console.log(ctx.request.href);
// => http://localhost:1234/?param=1
```

- request.path: This returns the request pathname. An example request to http://localhost:1234/hello would give the following:

```
console.log(ctx.request.path);
// => /hello
```

- request.querystring: This returns the raw query string without the prepending ?.
- request.querystring=: This sets the request raw query string.
- request.search: This returns the request raw query string, along with the prepending ?.

- request.search=: This sets the request raw query string.

- request.host: This returns the request host (hostname:port). It supports the X-Forwarded-Host header when app.proxy is set to true; otherwise, it defaults to the Host header:

```
console.log(ctx.request.host);
// => localhost:1234
```

- `request.hostname`: This returns the request hostname when present. This also supports the `X-Forwarded-Host` header when `app.proxy` is set to `true`. If the host is IPv6, Koa delegates the parsing to the WHATWG URL API (`https://nodejs.org/dist/latest-v8.x/docs/api/url.html#url_the_whatwg_url_api`). Delegating the parsing to the WHATWG URL API may affect performance.

- `request.URL`: This returns the WHATWG (`https://nodejs.org/dist/latest-v8.x/docs/api/url.html#url_the_whatwg_url_api`) parsed URL object.

- `request.type`

This returns the value of the `Content-Type` header, if present, without parameters such as charset:

- `request.charset`

This returns the request charset if present. Its default value is `undefined`:

- `request.query`: This returns the parsed query string from a request. A request to `http://localhost:1234/?param1=1&param2=2` would give the following:

```
console.log(ctx.request.query);
// => { param1: '1', param2: '2' }
```

This getter does not support nested object parsing.

- `request.query=`: This method is used to set the query string to a supplied object:

```
ctx.query = Object.assign(ctx.query, { param3: 3 });
console.log(ctx.request.query);
// => { param1: '1', param2: '2', param3: '3' }
```

This setter does not support nested objects.

- `request.fresh`: This is used to check whether the contents of a request cache have not changed, as shown here:

```
// check if cache is fresh
if (ctx.request.fresh) {
  ctx.status = 304;
  return;
}

// cache is stale, return data
ctx.body = "some data";
```

- `request.stale`: This is the inverse of the `request.fresh` method. It checks whether the contents of a request cache have changed.

- `request.protocol`: This returns the request protocol—`http` or `https`. This supports the `X-Forwarded-Host` header when `app.proxy` is set to `true`.

- `request.secure`: This simply returns a Boolean that is true when the request protocol is `https` and false when it's `http` as shown here:

```
// https://example.com
console.log(ctx.request.secure);
// => true

// http://example.com
console.log(ctx.request.secure);
// => false
```

- `request.ip`: This returns the request remote address. This supports `X-Forwarded-Host` when `app.proxy` is set to `true`.

- `request.ips`: This returns an array of IPs from upstream to downstream, when the `X-Forwarded-Host` header is set and `app.proxy` is set to `true`. It returns an empty array otherwise.

- `request.subdomains`: This returns the sub-domains on the request as an array. A good illustration of the behavior of this getter can be seen in the Koa docs:

"For example, if the domain is `"tobi.ferrets.example.com"`*: If app.subdomainOffset is not set,* `ctx.subdomains` *is* `["ferrets", "tobi"]`*. If* `app.subdomainOffset` *is 3,* `ctx.subdomains` *is* `["tobi"]`*."*

- `request.is(types...)`: This checks the value of the `Content-Type` header and compares it to the values of the types supplied to find a match. If it finds a match, it returns the matching `Content-Type`. If no request body is not present, it returns `null`. If no `Content-Type` is present, or the match fails, then it returns `false`:

```
// With Content-Type as text/html
console.log(ctx.is('html'));
// => 'html'
console.log(ctx.is('text/html'));
// => 'text/html'
console.log(ctx.is('text/*', 'text/html'));
// => 'text/html'
```

Content negotiation

The Koa request object includes some helper methods for content negotiation, powered by `accepts` and `negotiator`. These include the following:

- `request.accepts(types...)`: This checks whether the given types are acceptable, then returns the best match when true. It returns false if the types are not acceptable. The `types` value may be a comma separated list of mime type strings or extension names, or an array. This is shown in the following block:

```
// Accept: text/*, application/json
ctx.accepts('text/html');
// => "text/html"
ctx.accepts(['html', 'json']);
// => "json"
ctx.accepts('png');
// => false
```

- `request.acceptsEncodings(encodings)`: This checks whether the `encodings` supplied are acceptable and returns the best match when true. It returns `false` when no match exists. It returns all the accepted encodings as an array when no argument is given, as shown here:

```
// Accept-Encoding: gzip, deflate, br
ctx.acceptsEncodings()
// => [ 'gzip', 'deflate', 'br', 'identity' ]
```

- `request.acceptsLanguages(langs)`: This checks whether the `langs` supplied are accepted and returns the best match when `true`. It returns `false` when no match exists. It returns all the accepted languages as an array when no argument is given:

```
// Accept-Language: en-US,en;q=0.9,cy;q=0.8

console.log(ctx.acceptsLanguages('en'));
// => en

console.log(ctx.acceptsLanguages('en', 'cy'));
// => en
console.log(ctx.acceptsLanguages(['en', 'cy']));
// => en

ctx.acceptsLanguages();
// => [ 'en-US', 'en', 'cy' ]

console.log(ctx.acceptsLanguages('es'));
// => false
```

- `request.idempotent`: This returns a Boolean specifying whether the request is idempotent or not.

  A request is idempotent if multiple identical requests with that method have the same effect on the server as the effect for a single such request.

- `request.socket`: This returns the request socket.

- `request.get(field)`: This returns the request header value for a specified field:

```
// Accept-Language: en-US,en;q=0.9,cy;q=0.8

ctx.request.get('Accept-Language');
// => en-US,en;q=0.9,cy;q=0.8
```

The response object

The Koa response object is an abstraction of Node's response object. Like the request object, it provides added functionality with its properties and methods for building out everyday HTTP servers.

The methods and properties it exposes include the following:

- `response.header`: This returns the response header object.

- `response.headers`: This returns the response header object. It is an alias of `response.header`.

- `response.socket`: This returns the request socket.

- `response.status`: This returns the response status code, which is 404 by default. This is in contrast to Vanilla Node, where the default status for `res.statusCode` is 200.

- `response.status=`: This is used to set the response status code to a valid HTTP numeric status code.

- `response.message`: This returns the response status message. By default, this is associated with the `response.status`:

```
ctx.response.status = 202;
console.log(ctx.response.message);
// => Accepted
```

- `response.message=`: This is used to set the response status message to the supplied value.

- `response.length=`: This is used to set the response `Content-Length` header value to the given value.

- `response.length`: This returns the `Content-Length` as a number when available. It can also return the length by evaluating the content from the `ctx.body` when possible. It returns undefined when both the `Content-Length` and `ctx.body` are unavailable.

- `response.body`: This returns the response body. Popularly aliased as `ctx.body`.

- `response.body=`: This sets the response body to one of the following:
  - String
  - Buffer
  - Stream
  - Object/Array
  - Null

- `response.get(field)`: This returns the value of the field header. The field comparison is case-insensitive, as shown:

```
ctx.body = 'Hello World';
console.log(ctx.response.get('content-length'));
// => 11
```

- `response.set(field, value)`: This is used to set the response header `field` to a defined `value` as shown here:

```
ctx.set('Content-Language', 'en');
```

- `response.append(field, value)`: This appends an additional header `field` with a `value`.

- `response.set(fields)`: This sets several response header `fields` as an object as shown:

```
ctx.set({
   'Content-Language': 'en',
   'Retry-After': 120
});
```

- `response.remove(field)`: This removes a header field.

- `response.type`: This returns the response `Content-Type`.

- `response.type=`: This sets the `Content-Type` via mime string or file extension.

- `response.is(types...)`: This checks whether the response type is one of the `types` specified.

- `response.redirect(url, [alt])`: This performs a 302 permanent redirect to a specified `url`. The string `back` provides referrer support. When the referrer is not present, `alt` or / is used.

To alter the default 302 status, assign the status before or after the redirect call. To alter the response body, assign it after the call:

```
ctx.response.status = 301;
ctx.redirect('back');
ctx.body = "redirecting you to the previous page...";
```

- `response.attachment([filename])`: This sets the `Content-Disposition` to `attachment` and optionally specifies the `filename`. Setting the `Content-Disposition` to attachment readies the client to receive the response as a download.

- `response.headerSent`: This returns a Boolean specifying if a response header has already been sent.

- `response.lastModified`: This returns the `Last-Modified` header as a `Date` if it exists.

- `response.lastModified=`: This sets the last-modified to a UTC string. This method can either be supplied a `Date` object or a simple date string.

- `response.etag=`: This sets the ETag header to a specified value.

- `response.vary(field)`: This is used to set the value of the `Vary` header to a specified field.

- `response.flushHeaders()`: This method flushes any set headers and begins the response body.

Middleware

Middleware functions are a common concept in modern web development. A middleware function is one that has access to both the request and response objects in an application and can run the subsequent middleware after it is processed.

Middleware creation and registration in Koa is straightforward and is one of the reasons the framework is so widely adopted.

Cascading in Koa

Koa takes advantage of async functions to make middleware functions run in a truly cascaded fashion. The registered middlewares run in a stack-like manner and run from one level to the other until there is no other middleware to run.

The use of async functions is an improvement over other frameworks that have tried to implement stack-like middleware, as callbacks in Node made it much harder. Koa contrasts Connect, for example, in that Connect simply passes control through a series of functions until one returns. In Koa, the middleware functions are invoked *downstream*, and the control flows back *upstream*.

Here is an example from the Koa documentation showing the use of middleware:

```
const Koa = require('koa');
const app = new Koa();

// logger
app.use(async (ctx, next) => {
  await next();
  const rt = ctx.response.get('X-Response-Time');
  console.log(`${ctx.method} ${ctx.url} - ${rt}`);
});

// x-response-time
app.use(async (ctx, next) => {
  const start = Date.now();
  await next();
  const ms = Date.now() - start;
  ctx.set('X-Response-Time', `${ms}ms`);
});

// response
app.use(async ctx => {
  ctx.body = 'Hello World';
});

app.listen(3000);
```

In the preceding code block, the request first flows through the `logger` middleware, and then the `x-response-time` middleware, which marks when the request started, and finally the response middleware, which sends the `Hello World` response. When a middleware calls `next()`, the middleware function suspends and passes control to the next middleware defined. Once no other middleware exists to execute downstream, the stack will unwind and each middleware is resumed to perform its upstream behavior.

Defining middleware

Defining a middleware function in Koa involves creating an asynchronous function with two arguments—the context object (`ctx`), and the next method (`next`), which invokes the `next` middleware function to be called. This is similar to the way middleware functions are defined in Express. One major difference in their approach is that Koa implements the context object in place of the individual request (`req`) and response (`res`) objects provided by Node. Another difference is that Koa makes use of the `async... await` paradigm in place of callback functions.

Let's define a simple middleware to log how long it takes our application to process requests. In the following code block, we define a middleware function, and in the next section, we will register it and get to see it in action:

```
const responseTimer = async (ctx, next) => {
  const { method, path } = ctx.request;
  const start = Date.now();
  await next();
  const timeTaken = (Date.now() - start) / 1000; // divide by 1000 to get
time in seconds
  console.log(`${method} request to ${path} took ${timeTaken}s`);
};
```

Registering middleware

Registering middleware in Koa is done with the `.use()` method found in the application object. To register the middleware defined in the previous section:

```
app.use(responseTimer);
```

 Ensure you pass in the function reference when registering the middleware, and not call the function instead. A common mistake is to pass in `responseTimer()` instead of `responseTimer`.

Next, we can define and register a middleware to send a response back for every route as shown here:

```
// ...

app.use(async ctx => {
  ctx.body = 'Hello World';
});
```

The complete application will look like this:

```
// koa-middleware.js

// initialize Koa
const Koa = require('koa');
const app = new Koa();

// create middleware function
const responseTimer = async (ctx, next) => {
  const { method, path } = ctx.request;
  const start = Date.now();
  await next();
  const timeTaken = (Date.now() - start) / 1000; // divide by 1000 to get
time in seconds
  console.log(`${method} request to ${path} took ${timeTaken}s`);
};

// register middleware
app.use(responseTimer);

// send response back
app.use(async ctx => {
  ctx.body = 'Hello World';
});

// start application
app.listen(1234, () => {
  console.log('Server is running on port 1234')
});
```

Next, we can run the app with the following command:

```
node koa-middleware.js
```

Making a request to an endpoint on the application would produce logs such as this on your console:

```
GET request to / took 0.023s
GET request to /robots.txt took 0s
```

Common middleware

Some common middleware used in everyday application development in Koa includes the following:

- `koa-router`: RESTful resource router for Koa
- `koa-connect`: For mounting connect/express middleware
- `kcors`: For CORS support
- `koa-body`: For parsing HTTP request body
- `koa-logger`: Development style logger for Koa

A comprehensive list of supported middleware can be found on Koa's `middleware wiki`.

Summary

In this chapter, we took a comprehensive look into the inner workings of Koa with a focus on its context, request, and response objects. We learned about the APIs for these objects and the methods and properties that they expose.

We also discussed middleware functions in Koa. We learned how to create and register middleware functions. We also looked into some popular middleware already available in the Koa ecosystem.

In the next chapter, we will learn about errors in Koa and discuss the best methods for error handling.

4
Handling Errors in Koa

Error handling describes how your application responds to errors that occur in your application. It is an important part of software development; hence, developers spend a lot of time trying to handle errors properly. It is important to note that these errors may either be asynchronous or synchronous. Proper error handling by developers makes use of their applications more seamless.

Koa's use of asynchronous functions makes error handling easier than it is in other Node frameworks, which implement callbacks.

In this chapter, we will learn about error handling in Koa and how we can take advantage of the tooling in Koa for proper error handling. Some of the things we will learn in this chapter include the following:

- Catching errors in Koa
- The error event and listener
- Throwing HTTP errors
- Writing error handlers

Technical requirements

Similarly to the previous chapter, to follow along with this chapter, you need the following installed locally:

- **Node.js (>= v7.6.0) and NPM**: You can find download and installation instructions for this on the Node.js official website (`https://nodejs.org/en/`).
- **MongoDB**: This is one of the most popular NoSQL databases in the world. It is open source, and you can find download instructions on its official website (`https://www.mongodb.com/`) as well.

If you use macOS, you can make use of the Homebrew package manager to install Node.js and MongoDB easily.

The code files of this chapter can be found on GitHub:
`https://github.com/PacktPublishing/Server-Side-development-with-Node.js-and-Koa.js-Quick-Start-Guide/tree/master/Chapter04`

Check out the following video to see the code in action:
`http://bit.ly/2P8pfxv`

Catching errors in Koa

One of the great things about error handling in Koa is that, by default, the framework handles all errors, either asynchronous or synchronous. This is made possible by the fact that Koa has a cascading middleware stack and an error handler can be added at the very top of the stack, which will unwind last. This makes it possible for Koa to handle all uncaught errors in applications by default.

Koa's default behavior is to output all errors to stderr unless `app.silent` is set to `true`.

To catch errors that occur in Koa, you can define an error-handling middleware to run as one of the first middleware. This is in contrast to Express, where error-handling middleware has to be defined as the last in the stack, with the signature `(err, req, res, next)`.

In Koa, error-handling middleware can be defined as any other middleware, with the notable exception that it has to be registered as one of the first middleware. This ensures that the handler catches all errors in subsequent middleware.

A simple handler can be defined as seen as follows:

```
// catch all error in preceding middleware
app.use(async (ctx, next) => {
  try {
    await next();
  } catch(err) {
    ctx.status = err.status || 500;
    ctx.body = err.message;
  }
});

// throw error in response middleware
app.use(async ctx => {
  throw new Error('An error occurred');
  ctx.body = 'Hello, world';
});
```

In the code block, first, we define and register a middleware that wraps the call to the next `middleware` function in a `try` block. Hence, all errors that are thrown in subsequent middleware cascade up and will flow into the corresponding `catch` block.

Running the preceding code in a Koa app and visiting any route in the app will write a text response back to the client with the `An error occurred` message:

```
curl http://localhost:1234

// => An error occurred
```

Koa makes it possible to use simple `try... catch` statements for error handling, unlike in Express where the error in asynchronous functions has to be explicitly passed to the next middleware, using the `next()` method.

Errors can also be caught and transformed by implementing error-handling middleware. This is particularly useful for transforming errors of a particular kind and can help to reduce multiple `try... catch` statements. Here is an example of this use case:

```
app.use(async (ctx, next) => {
  try {
    await next();
  } catch(err) {
    if (err.status === 409 || err.statusCode === 409) {
      err.message = "Conflict with current data exists!"
    }
    throw err;
  }
});
```

In the preceding example, the error is modified and throw again to be handled by Koa's default response handler.

Koa's default error handler

Koa implements a default error handler, which works well for many situations. It is essentially middleware with a `try...catch` statement defined at the very top of the Koa middleware stack. If no other error handler is defined, all errors thrown when the application is running will flow into Koa's default error handler.

The default handler uses the status code of `err.status` when available, else it uses `500` (for `Internal Server Error`). It also sends back `err.message` as the response if `err.expose` is set to `true`.

If `err.expose` is set to `false`, then it generates a message from the error code of the error thrown. For example, for the `400 Bad Request` error, the message generated will be `Invalid Request`.

When sending back a response, the default error handler clears all headers, except for the ones present in `err.headers`. We can set headers for errors using a `try...catch` statement in another middleware, as seen here:

```
app.use(async (ctx, next) => {
  try {
    await next();
  } catch(err) {
    if (err.status === 503) {
      err.headers = Object.assign({}, err.headers, {
        'Retry-After': 30
      });
    }

    throw err;
  }
});
```

The preceding code shows how we set the `Retry-After` header value for `503 Service Unavailable` errors.

When an error occurs, and it is still possible to respond back to the client (no data has been written to the socket), as expected, Koa responds with `500 Internal Server Error`. Either way, the error event is still emitted.

Emitting errors

It is recommended that you emit an error on the application itself. This is useful for centralized error reporting or logging. This also helps to retain the default behavior of Koa for errors. Errors can be emitted using the `ctx.app.emit()` method:

```
app.use(async (ctx, next) => {
  try {
    await next();
  } catch (err) {
    ctx.status = err.status || 500;
    ctx.body = err.message;
    ctx.app.emit('error', err, ctx);
  }
});
```

Error event listener

Error event listeners can be defined with `app.on('error')`. They are particularly useful for centralized logging and error reporting. The error listeners receive all errors that are thrown in the middleware chain, except the ones that are caught and are neither rethrown or emitted using `app.emit()`. To define an error handler, refer to this code:

```
app.on('error', err => {
  // log errors
  console.error("server error", err);
});
```

If no event listener is defined, then `app.onerror` is used. This simply outputs the error to `stdout` unless `app.silent` is `true`, `err.status` is `404`, or `err.expose` is set to `true`.

If an error is thrown in the middleware chain and it is not possible to respond to the client, the context object is also passed to the event listener:

```
app.on('error', (err, ctx) => {
  console.error("server error", err, ctx);
});
```

It is important to note that these are user-level errors and are therefore safe to expose to the user (`err.expose` is set to `true`). This is usually not the case for all error messages, especially with 50x errors, where we do not want to show the client sensitive information from failures.

Throwing HTTP errors

Koa provides a helper method for easily throwing errors with appropriate HTTP status codes. It uses `http-errors` for error creation. The `ctx.throw()` method throws an error with a `.status` property, which is `500` (`Internal Server Error`) by default. This error with the status property enables Koa to respond properly when different errors occur. The method has the signature, `ctx.throw([status], [error], [properties])`. The following different usages are permitted:

```
ctx.throw(401);
ctx.throw(401, 'Access denied to the resource');
ctx.throw(401, 'Access denied to the resource', { user });
```

Throwing `ctx.throw(401, 'Access denied to the resource')`, for example, is shorthand for the following:

```
const err = new Error('Access denied to the resource');
err.status = 401;
err.expose = true;
throw err;
```

It is important to note that these errors are OK for sending to the user, meaning `err.expose` is set to `true`. This is usually not the case, especially for 50x errors, where we would not want sensitive details about our app failures to be shown to users, who could possibly be malicious.

The `.throw()` method also optionally take a properties object that is merged into the error as is. This can be used for passing extra information, which is reported to the requested upstream and can also be used for creating better error messages:

```
app.use(async ctx => {
    ctx.throw(401, 'Access denied to the resource', { user });
});
```

The error thrown in the preceding code block can be used for creating better error messages, as seen in the following example:

```
app.use(async (ctx, next) => {
  try {
    await next();
  } catch(err) {
    ctx.body = err.message;
    if (err.status === 401) {
        const { email } = err.user;
        ctx.body = `user with email ${email} does not have access to
        resource`;
    }
  }
});
```

Note that you can only throw error status codes. These include 4xx and 5xx status code.

Here is a list of the supported status codes:

- 400: Bad Request
- 401: Unauthorized
- 402: Payment Required
- 403: Forbidden
- 404: Not Found
- 405: Method Not Allowed
- 406: Not Acceptable
- 407: Proxy Authentication Required
- 408: Request Timeout
- 409: Conflict
- 410: Gone
- 411: Length Required
- 412: Precondition Failed
- 413: Payload Too Large
- 414: URI Too Long
- 415: Unsupported Media Type
- 416: Range Not Satisfiable
- 417: Expectation Failed
- 418: I'm A Teapot
- 421: Misdirected Request
- 422: UnprocessableEntity
- 423: Locked
- 424: FailedDependency
- 425: Unordered Collection
- 426: Upgrade Required
- 428: Precondition Required
- 429: Too Many Requests

- 431: Request Header Fields Too Large
- 451: Unavailable For Legal Reasons
- 500: Internal Server Error
- 501: Not Implemented
- 502: Bad Gateway
- 503: Service Unavailable
- 504: Gateway Timeout
- 505: HTTP Version Not Supported
- 506: Variant Also Negotiates
- 507: Insufficient Storage
- 508: Loop Detected
- 509: Bandwidth Limit Exceeded
- 510: Not Extended
- 511: Network Authentication Required

 Note that 5xx status code errors do not expose the error message to the response body in Koa.

Writing error handlers

To register custom error handlers in Koa, we simply need to define middleware with a `try... catch` statement to capture the errors, then send responses back to the client. This should be done at the top of the stack.

We can define error handlers based on various requirements to handle different types of errors for different types of clients. These error handlers can be used independently or combined, depending on the needs of the application. Let's define a set of error handlers and register them in our application:

```
const jsonErrorHandler = async (ctx, next) => {
  try {
    await next();
  } catch (err) {
    const isJson = ctx.get('Accept') === 'application/json';
    if (isJson) {
      ctx.body = {
        error: 'An error just occurred'
      }
```

```
  } else {
    throw err;
  }
  }
}


app.use(jsonErrorHandler);
```

The first error handler defined is for catching errors on Ajax requests or requests that only accept JSON responses.

Next, we can define a catch-all error handler. This can be substituted with an error page in a real-life application:

```
const errorHandler = async (ctx, next) => {
  try {
    await next();
  } catch (err) {
    ctx.status = err.status || 500;
    ctx.body = err.expose ? err.message : 'An error occurred!';
  }
}


app.use(errorHandler);
```

Putting both error handlers together, they will look like the code block below:

```
// define generic error handler
const errorHandler = async (ctx, next) => {
  try {
    await next();
  } catch (err) {
    ctx.status = err.status || 500;
    ctx.body = err.expose ? err.message : 'An error occurred!';
  }
}


// register generic error handler middleware
app.use(errorHandler);


// define json request error handler
const jsonErrorHandler = async (ctx, next) => {
  try {
    await next();
  } catch (err) {
    const isJson = ctx.get('Accept') === 'application/json';
    if (isJson) {
      ctx.status = err.status || 500;
```

```
        ctx.body = {
            error: `An error just occurred`
        }
    } else {
        throw err;
    }
  }
}

// register json error handler middleware
app.use(jsonErrorHandler);
```

 Note: We register the generic handler first, as it will be the last
middleware to be executed as the middleware stack unwinds.

Summary

In this chapter, we have learned how error handling in Koa works out of the box. We have
learned, with code examples, how to define and register our own custom error-handling
middleware. We also learned about the error event in Koa and how to define listeners for
centralized logging and other purposes.

The use of `async... await` in Koa makes error handling a lot easier than in traditional
middleware-based frameworks, as we simply have to define `try... catch` statements to
do most of the heavy lifting.

Proper error handling is a must-have for almost all applications going into production. This
is another reason why Koa is such a great choice for production-grade HTTP applications.

In the next chapter, we will be building a Koa application from scratch, and we will utilize
all the information we have learned from the previous lessons.

5
Building an API in Koa

Web **application programming interfaces** (**APIs**) have become more and more popular, as more people have started to recognize the need to separate their server-side applications from their client-side applications. APIs give developers the opportunity to offer the same web services to multiple clients, while also reducing the coupling between their systems.

In this chapter, we will build a REST API using Koa. We will make use of the different Koa concepts that we covered in the previous chapters in order to build a full-fledged API.

The API that we will build will be for managing contacts. We will be able to perform **create, read, update, and delete (CRUD)** operations on contacts in our database via the API. We will persist and retrieve data to and from a MongoDB database, using Mongoose. We will also make use of Nodemon to debug our applications, and Postman to test our APIs.

Through building the API, you will learn about the following topics:

- How to build a CRUD service in Koa
- How to send JSON data back as a response
- How to structure an API in Koa
- How to implement logging for all requests that are made
- How to set up routing in a Koa application
- How to retrieve and process request body data in Koa
- How to implement validation in Node APIs
- How to define and implement custom middleware in a real-world application

 All of the code written in this chapter uses the modern JavaScript ES6 syntax.

Technical requirements

To follow along with this chapter, you will need the following installed on your local machine:

- **Node.js (version 7.6.0, or higher) and NPM**: You can find download and installation instructions on the Node.js official website (`https://nodejs.org/en/`).
- **MongoDB**: This is one of the most popular NoSQL databases in the world. It is open source, and you can find download instructions on its official website, as well (`https://www.mongodb.com/`).
- Postman: This is a tool for testing web APIs. It is available for download on different platforms (`https://www.getpostman.com/apps`).

 Note: If you use macOS, you can make use of the Homebrew package manager to easily install Node.js and MongoDB.

The code files of this chapter can be found on GitHub:
`https://github.com/PacktPublishing/Server-Side-development-with-Node.js-and-Koa.js-Quick-Start-Guide/tree/master/Chapter05`

Check out the following video to see the code in action:
`http://bit.ly/2zveHnq`

Project setup

Once we have all of the prerequisite software installed, we can start to develop our project locally. The first thing that we need to do is initialize our `Node.js` project.

Initialization

Most modern JavaScript projects and packages have a `package.json` file. This file specifies various metadata about the project, including the following:

- Dependencies
- Descriptions
- Repository information

- Config information
- Common scripts

To initialize our project and create a `package.json` file, we will run the following command:

```
npm init
```

After running the command, a prompt will show up, asking us to fill in some details about the project.

 Note: To initialize a project with default values, you can run the `npm init` command with the `-y` flag: `npm init -y`.

Installing dependencies

To run our application properly, we need some external dependencies. We can get these dependencies by using a package manager, like `npm` or `yarn`.

Some of the packages that we need are as follows:

- `koa`: Our base framework
- `koa-router`: RESTful routing middleware for Koa
- `koa-logger`: Development-style logger middleware for Koa
- `koa-body`: Request body parser middleware for Koa
- `mongoose`: **Object data modelling (ODM)** library for MongoDB and Node.js
- `joi`: Object schema validation library

To install these dependencies into our application using `npm`, we use the following command:

```
npm install --save koa koa-router koa-logger koa-body mongoose joi
```

The `--save` flag specifies that we want to save these packages as dependencies in our `package.json` file.

With newer versions of npm, you do not need to specify the --save flag for installed packages to be added as dependencies in the package.json file. You can simply install and save dependencies with npm install or npm i.

Structure

We will structure our application in a simple and modular manner, following a slight modification of the MVC architectural pattern.

We will create controllers in a controllers folder, which will house the business logic for our application. Our data objects will also sit in a similarly named models folder. We will also create a middleware folder to house our application's middleware functions.

An index.js file will be created to serve as the entry point for our server. We will load up the required dependencies, configure our middleware, and start our server from this file.

To create the required folders, we can run the following command in the Terminal:

```
mkdir controllers middleware models
```

To create the entry point file, we can run the following command in the Terminal:

```
touch index.js
```

After initialization, and having created the required folders and files, the structure should look as follows:

```
├── controllers
├── index.js
├── middleware
├── models
├── package-lock.json
└── package.json
```

Building the application

In this section, we will get right into the code and start to build our application. We will need to follow these steps:

1. Starting the server
2. Connecting to a database

3. Creating data models
4. Setting up a router
5. Setting up a logger
6. Creating contact endpoints and controller actions
7. Validating requests

Starting the server

First, let's start a simple server in our `index.js` entry file. In the following code block, we simply require Koa as a dependency, then start a Koa server by using the `app.listen()` method:

```
// ./index.js

const Koa = require('koa');
const app = new Koa();

const port = process.env.PORT || 3000;
app.listen(port, () =>
  console.log(`Server running on http://localhost:${port}`)
);
```

The server either runs on a specified port with the `PORT` environmental variable, or on the default `3000` port.

To start our application, you can run the following command from the project root:

```
node index.js
```

You should see the following message in your console after running this: `Server running on http://localhost:3000`.

To start the application on a different port, you can specify the following `PORT` environment variable when starting the application:

```
PORT=1234 node index.js
```

Running this will produce the following message: `Server running on http://localhost:1234`.

Using Nodemon

Nodemon is a command-line tool that helps with the speedy development of Node.js applications. It monitors your project directory and automatically restarts your node application when it detects any changes.

This means that you do not have to stop and restart your applications in order for your changes to take effect. You can simply write code, and test your application a few seconds later.

To install nodemon locally, we can run the following in the Terminal::

```
npm install -g nodemon
```

Nodemon serves as a replacement for node, and does not require any code changes within your application. Once it has installed, we can start our application with auto-restart, using the following command:

```
nodemon index.js
```

You can also try to run the following command:

```
PORT=1234 nodemon index.js
```

Now, after making a change to any file in your project directory, nodemon will automatically restart your server, and you will get to see the changes in effect.

Connecting to a database

MongoDB, the NoSQL database, which is popular for being a part of the **MEAN stack** (**MongoDB, Express, Angular, and Node.js**), will be used to persist all of our contact data into our API. Its ability to easily save JSON objects without needing a strict schema setup is great for our purposes.

We will be making use of Mongoose, a popular ODM library, for all of our database interactions. Mongoose manages our interactions with the database, does object schema validation, and also maps objects in our code into their corresponding MongoDB document representations.

Let's update our `index.js` file, in order to allow our app to connect to the database with Mongoose, as follows:

```
// ./index.js
// ...

const mongoose = require('mongoose');
mongoose.connect(
  'mongodb://localhost:27017/koa-contact',
  { useNewUrlParser: true }
);

const db = mongoose.connection;
db.on('error', error => {
  throw new Error(`error connecting to db: ${error}`);
});
db.once('open', () => console.log('database connected'));

// ...
```

In the preceding code block, first, we require the `mongoose` dependency as the `mongoose` object. Then, we use the `mongoose.connect()` method to connect our Mongo database. The `connect` method takes the MongoDB connection URL as its first argument, then an object with connection options as its second. The only option that we specify is for `mongoose` to use the new URL parser for the mongo connection string.

Next, we define listeners to alert us when there's an error connecting to the DB, and once the database is successfully connected to.

At this point, the complete `index.js` file should look as follows:

```
// ./index.js

// require needed dependencies
const Koa = require('koa');
const app = new Koa();

// connect to mongodb with mongoose
const mongoose = require('mongoose');
mongoose.connect(
  'mongodb://localhost:27017/koa-contact',
  { useNewUrlParser: true }
);

// listen for successful connection, or error
const db = mongoose.connection;
db.on('error', error => {
```

```
    throw new Error(`error connecting to db: ${error}`);
});
db.once('open', () => console.log('database connected'));

// start server
const port = process.env.PORT || 3000;
app.listen(port, () =>
  console.log(`Server running on http://localhost:${port}`)
);
```

Running this, you should see a `database connected` message on your console or Terminal, right after the server starts.

Creating data models

To communicate with our database, we need to define a data model for the contacts. Mongoose models serve as wrappers around schema definitions. A Mongoose schema defines the object structure, constraints, default values, and so on. Models are responsible for CRUD operations for an object with the underlying database.

To create a simple data model, let's create a `Contact.js` file in the `models` folder, and insert the following code into it:

```
// ./models/Contact.js

const Koa = require('koa');
const app = new Koa();

const mongoose = require('mongoose');
mongoose.connect(
  'mongodb://localhost:27017/koa-contact',
  { useNewUrlParser: true }
);

const db = mongoose.connection;
db.on('error', error => {
  throw new Error(`error connecting to db: ${error}`);
});
db.once('open', () => console.log('database connected'));

const port = process.env.PORT || 3000;
app.listen(port, () =>
  console.log(`Server running on http://localhost:${port}`)
);
```

In the preceding code block, first, we require the `mongoose` dependency. The `mongoose` reference that is created here will be the same as the one that was returned when we initially connected to the database. This means that we do not need to create any other connections for interacting with our database.

Next, we define our schema by using the `mongoose.Schema` object. Our contact object will have the following properties:

- `name`: The name of a contact. This should be a string. This is a required value, and the schema validation will fail if a contact object without a name is persisted to the database.
- `company`: The company that a contact works at. This should be a string value.
- `position`: The position that a contact holds at a company. Also a string value.
- `address`: The contact's address. Also a string value.
- `phoneNumber`: The contact's phone number. This is also specified as a string value, to cater to special characters, such as a country code or parentheses.
- `createdAt`: The date that the document was created. This can be saved as a JavaScript date object. The default value is the current date.
- `updatedAt`: The date that the document was most recently updated. This can be saved as a JavaScript date object. The default value is the current date.

Finally, we will create the mongoose model and export it, so that it can be used elsewhere in our application.

Setting up the router

In order to be able to visit different endpoints, we need to set up some form of a router, to route different URL oath visits to different actions. Koa does not come bundled with an out-of-the-box router like Express does; hence, we will be making use of `koa-router`, which is an open source RESTful router for use with Koa.

Let's start off by creating a `router.js` file in the `middleware` folder, and inserting the following contents:

```
// ./middleware/router.js

const KoaRouter = require('koa-router');
const router = new KoaRouter();

router
  .get('/', async ctx => (ctx.body = 'Welcome to the contacts API!'));

module.exports = router;
```

In the preceding code block, we require the `koa-router` dependency, and we initialize it. After that, we register an index route, which sends the `Welcome to the contacts API!` text response. Then, we export it to be registered as a middleware in our index file.

To define a route, we call the HTTP verb method of the router, which takes the route path as the first parameter, and a callback function as the second. For example, for a GET route, we use `router.get()`; for a POST route, we use `router.post()`; and so on.

Update the `index.js` file, as follows:

```
// ./index.js

// ...
const router = require('./middleware/router');

// router
app.use(router.routes());
app.use(router.allowedMethods());

// ...
```

After requiring the router middleware, we register it with the `router.routes()` and `router.allowedMethods()` methods. The `.routes()` method registers the routes that we define via the router, and the `.allowedMethods()` method returns a separate middleware for responding to the `OPTIONS` requests, with the `Allow` header containing the allowed methods.

Our complete `index.js` file will now look as follows:

```
const Koa = require('koa');
const router = require('./middleware/router');
const app = new Koa();

const mongoose = require('mongoose');
mongoose.connect(
  'mongodb://localhost:27017/koa-contact',
  { useNewUrlParser: true }
);

const db = mongoose.connection;
db.on('error', error => {
  throw new Error(`error connecting to db: ${error}`);
});
db.once('open', () => console.log('database connected'));

// router
app.use(router.routes());
app.use(router.allowedMethods());

const port = process.env.PORT || 3000;
app.listen(port, () =>
  console.log(`Server running on http://localhost:${port}`)
);
```

With the router middleware and the routes registered, we can test the GET / route with Postman or a browser; we should see the **Welcome to the contacts API!** response, as shown in the following screenshot:

Setting up a logger

Sometimes, we need a logger to help with debugging during development. In this section, we will implement a simple Koa console logger, in order to log our requests to the console or Terminal.

It is recommended that the logger middleware be registered close to the top of the middleware stack, so that it can wrap all subsequent middleware.

To register the `koa-logger` middleware, refer to the following code block:

```
// ./index.js

// ...
const logger = require('koa-logger');

app.use(logger());

// ...
```

We can configure the logger with a custom transporter, as seen in the `koa-logger` documentation (https://github.com/koajs/logger).

Now, the `index.js` file, with the logger implemented, will look as follows:

```
// ./index.js

const Koa = require('koa');
const router = require('./middleware/router');
const app = new Koa();

const logger = require('koa-logger');

// logger
app.use(logger());

const mongoose = require('mongoose');
mongoose.connect(
  'mongodb://localhost:27017/koa-contact',
  { useNewUrlParser: true }
);

const db = mongoose.connection;
db.on('error', error => {
  throw new Error(`error connecting to db: ${error}`);
});
db.once('open', () => console.log('database connected'));
```

```
// router
app.use(router.routes());
app.use(router.allowedMethods());

const port = process.env.PORT || 3000;
app.listen(port, () =>
  console.log(`Server running on http://localhost:${port}`)
);
```

Now, when we run our app and hit the GET / endpoint, we will see the logs in the Terminal, showing request and response log data:

```
Server running on http://localhost:3000
database connected
  <-- GET /
  --> GET / 200 11ms
```

Creating contact endpoints and controller actions

Now that we have our model, our database connection, our router, and a logger setup, we can start to write the business logic for our application. This will mainly consist of different controller actions, to handle CRUD operations for the contacts in our database.

We will start by creating a ContactController.js file in the controllers folder, as follows:

```
touch controllers/ContactController.js
```

Next, we can define the different route actions in our controller.

Retrieving all contacts

The index route will retrieve all of the contacts from the database and send them back to the client in a JSON object. We can use the mongoose .find() method to retrieve all of the entries of a model from the database.

Insert the following code into the ContactController.js file:

```
// ./controllers/ContactController.js

const Contact = require('../models/Contact');

module.exports = {
  async index(ctx) {
```

```
        const contacts = await Contact.find();
        ctx.body = {
          status: 'success',
          data: contacts
        };
    }
};
```

Next, we head over to the `./middleware/router.js` file, in order to add the corresponding route, as follows:

```
// ./middleware/router.js
// ...
const contactController = require('../controllers/ContactController');

router
  .get('/', async ctx => (ctx.body = 'Welcome to the contacts API!'))
  .get('/contact', contactController.index);

//...
```

Calling the GET `/contact` endpoint should send a JSON object with a `success` status and an empty array as the data property. The data property, which is meant to hold a list of contacts, is empty, as we have not yet inserted any records into the database. An example response object can be seen as follows:

```
{
    "status": "success",
    "data": []
}
```

Storing new contacts

The `store` route will create new contact documents and save them to the database. It will send the created contacts back as a JSON response.

The `store` action will receive the JSON request body as data to use for creating the contact document. In order to be able to read the request body properly, we need to register koa-body, a body parser middleware for Koa.

According to its documentation, `koa-body` is the following:

> "*A full-featured Koa body parser middleware. Supports multipart,* `urlencoded` *and* `json` *request bodies. Provides same functionality as Express's bodyParser -* `multer`*. And all that is wrapped only around* `co-body` *and formidable.*"

The `koa-body` documentation (`https://github.com/dlau/koa-bod`) shows a lot of example usages and configuration options for implementing the middleware.

To register the `koa-body` middleware, we can update our `index.js` with the following content:

```
// ./index.js

// ...

const bodyParser = require('koa-body');

app.use(bodyParser());

// ...
```

To add the `store` route, we will update the controller actions, as follows:

```
// ./controllers/ContactController.js

// ...

module.exports = {
  // ...

  async store(ctx) {
    const { body } = ctx.request;
    let contact = new Contact(body);
    contact = await contact.save();
    ctx.body = {
      status: 'success',
      data: contact
    };
  }
};
```

Then, we register the corresponding route, as follows:

```
// ./middleware/router.js
// ...

router
  .get('/', async ctx => (ctx.body = 'Welcome to the contacts API!'))
  .get('/contact', contactController.index)
  .post('/contact', contactController.store);

// ...
```

Now, we can call the POST /contact endpoint to create a contact with Postman, as seen in the following screenshot:

Retrieving a single contact

The show route will retrieve a single contact from the database, via a specified id, and send it back as a response to the client. We can get the required id from the route parameter, and easily pass it to the mongoose .findById() method, in order to retrieve the required contact. We update the controller, as follows:

```
// ./controllers/ContactController.js

// ...

module.exports = {
  // ...

  async show(ctx) {
    const { id } = ctx.params;
    const contact = await Contact.findById(id);
    ctx.body = {
      status: 'success',
      data: contact
    };
  }
};
```

We then add the corresponding route, as follows:

```
// ./middleware/router.js
// ...

router
  .get('/', async ctx => (ctx.body = 'Welcome to the contacts API!'))
  .get('/contact', contactController.index)
  .post('/contact', contactController.store)
  .get('/contact/:id', contactController.show);

// ...
```

Making a request to retrieve a contact that we have already saved by calling `GET /contact/{contactId}` should return a response similar to the following:

```
{
    "status": "success",
    "data": {
        "_id": "5be8e3028053210ddc1d162b",
        "name": "Test name",
        "address": "Street 5",
        "company": "test company",
        "createdAt": "2018-11-12T02:18:42.377Z",
        "updatedAt": "2018-11-12T02:18:42.377Z",
        "__v": 0
    }
}
```

Updating a contact

The `update` route will update an existing contact with new details. We can achieve this by getting the required `id` as a route parameter, along with the updated content from the request body, then using the mongoose `.findByIdAndUpdate()` method to update the specified contact. The route will return the updated contact as a response on a successful update:

```
// ./controllers/ContactController.js

// ...

module.exports = {
  async index(ctx) {
    const contacts = await Contact.find();
    ctx.body = {
      status: 'success',
      data: contacts
    };
  },

  async store(ctx) {
    const { body } = ctx.request;
    let contact = new Contact(body);
    contact = await contact.save();
    ctx.body = {
      status: 'success',
      data: contact
    };
  },
```

```
  async show(ctx) {
    const { id } = ctx.params;
    const contact = await Contact.findById(id);
    ctx.body = {
      status: 'success',
      data: contact
    };
  },

  async update(ctx) {
    const { id } = ctx.params;
    const { body } = ctx.request;
    await Contact.findByIdAndUpdate(id, body);
    const contact = await Contact.findById(id);
    ctx.body = {
      status: 'success',
      message: 'contact successfully updated',
      data: contact
    };
  }
};
```

The corresponding router definition is shown as follows:

```
// ./middleware/router.js
// ...

router
  .get('/', async ctx => (ctx.body = 'Welcome to the contacts API!'))
  .get('/contact', contactController.index)
  .post('/contact', contactController.store)
  .get('/contact/:id', contactController.show)
  .put('/contact/:id', contactController.update);

// ...
```

An example request to `PUT /contact/{contactId}` to update a contact is shown in the following screenshot:

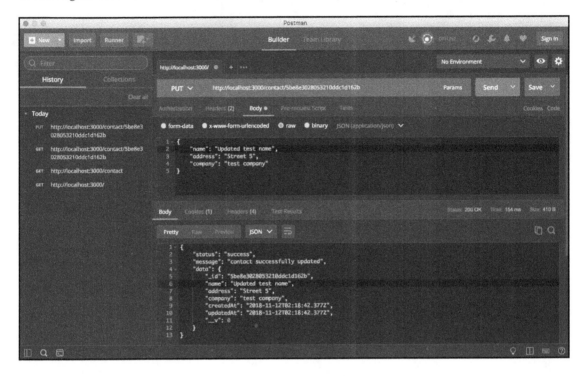

Deleting a contact

The `destroy` route will take an `id` route parameter and delete the contact with that `id` from the database, using the mongoose `.findByAndDelete()` method:

```js
// ./controllers/ContactController.js

// ...

module.exports = {
  async index(ctx) {
    const contacts = await Contact.find();
    ctx.body = {
      status: 'success',
      data: contacts
    };
  },
```

```
    async store(ctx) {
      const { body } = ctx.request;
      let contact = new Contact(body);
      contact = await contact.save();
      ctx.body = {
        status: 'success',
        data: contact
      };
    },

    async show(ctx) {
      const { id } = ctx.params;
      const contact = await Contact.findById(id);
      ctx.body = {
        status: 'success',
        data: contact
      };
    },

    async update(ctx) {
      const { id } = ctx.params;
      const { body } = ctx.request;
      await Contact.findByIdAndUpdate(id, body);
      const contact = await Contact.findById(id);
      ctx.body = {
        status: 'success',
        message: 'contact successfully updated',
        data: contact
      };
    },

    async destroy(ctx) {
      const { id } = ctx.params;
      await Contact.findByIdAndDelete(id);
      ctx.body = {
        status: 'success',
        message: 'contact successfully deleted'
      };
    }
};
```

We add the corresponding router definition, as follows:

```
// ./middleware/router.js
// ...

router
  .get('/', async ctx => (ctx.body = 'Welcome to the contacts API!'))
```

```
.get('/contact', contactController.index)
.post('/contact', contactController.store)
.get('/contact/:id', contactController.show)
.put('/contact/:id', contactController.update)
.delete('/contact/:id', contactController.destroy);

// ...
```

Making a request to `DELETE /contact/{contactId}` with the specified `id` should return a response similar to the following:

```
{
    "status": "success",
    "message": "contact successfully deleted"
}
```

Validating requests

A great way to ensure that we always get the data that we need is to validate requests before persisting them to the database. Mongoose already does schema validation, but we can also implement an extra layer of validation, to ensure that we are in full control of our data.

A popular JSON schema validation library that we can make use of in Node.js is `Joi`. `Joi` is an object schema validator, and it will work well for ensuring that we have the proper data coming through from our requests.

We will create a custom middleware for validating requests on selected routes, and register it in our app.

First, let's create the `middleware` function. Creating a `validator.js` file in the `middleware` folder can be done by using the following command:

```
touch middleware/validator.js
```

Now, we can insert the following content into the file:

```
// ./middleware/validator.js

const Joi = require('joi');

const schema = Joi.object({
 name: Joi.string().required(),
 address: Joi.string(),
 company: Joi.string(),
```

```
    position: Joi.string(),
    phoneNumber: Joi.number().required()
});

const ALLOWED_METHODS = ['PUT', 'POST'];

module.exports = () => {
  return async (ctx, next) => {
    const { method } = ctx;
    const { body } = ctx.request;

    if (ALLOWED_METHODS.includes(method)) {
      const { error } = Joi.validate(body, schema);
      if (error) {
        ctx.status = 422;
        ctx.body = {
          status: 'error',
          message: 'validation error',
          errors: error.details.map(e => e.message)
        };
      } else {
        await next();
      }
    } else {
      await next();
    }
  };
};
```

In the preceding code block, we specify the methods that we would like to validate against in the ALLOWED_METHODS variable. This ensures that we only validate against POST and PUT requests that contain request body data, and not GET requests, which do not. If a request matches any of these methods, we then validate the request body against a defined schema.

Joi possesses various methods for schema validation. Notably, we make use of the .required() method, to ensure that the name and phoneNumber properties are always present.

 Note that we only specify one validation schema in our application, as we only have one data model. In more complex applications, which possess multiple data models, multiple schemas need to be implemented, where the correct schema to use for validation can be decided based on the route.

If an error occurs from Joi during validation, we set the response status code to 422 (Unprocessable Entity) and send back the error messages from Joi.

To register the middleware, let's update the `index.js` file, as follows:

```
// ./index.js
// ...

const validator = require('./middleware/validator');

app.use(validator());

// ...
```

At this point, the complete `index.js` file looks as follows:

```
const Koa = require('koa');
const logger = require('koa-logger');
const bodyParser = require('koa-body');
const router = require('./middleware/router');
const validator = require('./middleware/validator');
const app = new Koa();

const mongoose = require('mongoose');
mongoose.connect(
  'mongodb://localhost:27017/koa-contact',
  { useNewUrlParser: true }
);

const db = mongoose.connection;
db.on('error', error => {
  throw new Error(`error connecting to db: ${error}`);
});
db.once('open', () => console.log('database connected'));

app.use(logger());

app.use(bodyParser());

app.use(validator());

app.use(router.routes());
app.use(router.allowedMethods());

const port = process.env.PORT || 3000;
app.listen(port, () =>
  console.log(`Server running on http://localhost:${port}`)
);
```

If we try to save a contact without specifying a name, the following is an example response that we might receive:

```
{
    "status": "error",
    "message": "validation error",
    "errors": [
        "\"name\" is required"
    ]
}
```

Useful notes

Some other important concepts to be conscious of when building APIs with Koa include the following:

- **Cross-origin resource sharing (CORS)**: Koa-cors is a great middleware that helps to enable CORS on Koa-built APIs. This ensures that you are able to connect to your API from other origins.
- Environment variables: You can environment variables, such as the port that you want the application to run in, database credentials, and so on, in a separate file, and load them into your variables by using the popular dotenv JavaScript module (`https://www.npmjs.com/package/dotenv`).

Summary

In this chapter, you learned how to build an API in Koa, from the ground up. You learned how to structure your projects in a modular manner when developing APIs in Koa. You also learned how to implement logging, routing, and validation on a CRUD API.

Koa shows us how easy it is to get started in API development, and we are really only limited by our imagination when it comes to building robust APIs with the framework.

In the next chapter, we will focus on building a blog with Koa. This will enable us to explore templating and authentication in Koa.

Building an Application in Koa

6

In this final chapter, we will be building a complete web application from scratch with Koa. This will help us to reinforce our learning and make use of concepts we have learned in a real-world application.

We will make use of all the concepts learned in previous chapters to build an end-to-end monolithic application in Koa.

Some of the things we will learn in this chapter include:

- How to build an end-to-end application from scratch with Koa
- How to handle sessions in Koa
- How to handle authentication in Koa
- How to create views and work with templates in Koa
- How to work with form data in Koa

Technical requirements

Similar to the previous chapter, to follow along with this chapter, you need the following installed locally:

- **Node.js (>= v7.6.0) and NPM**: You can find download and installation instructions for this on the Node.js official website.
- **MongoDB**: This is one of the most popular NoSQL databases in the world. It is open source, and you can find download instructions on its official website (https://www.mongodb.com/) as well.

If you use macOS, you can make use of the Homebrew package manager to install Node.js and MongoDB easily.

If you use macOS, you can make use of the Homebrew package manager to install Node.js and MongoDB easily.

The code files of this chapter can be found on GitHub:
`https://github.com/PacktPublishing/Server-Side-development-with-Node.js-and-Koa.js-Quick-Start-Guide/tree/master/Chapter06`

Check out the following video to see the code in action:
`http://bit.ly/2zzJcIN`

About the application

Some of the features our application will have include the following:

- Authentication to restrict access to some parts of the app
- The ability for users to log in, register, and logout
- Ability to serve HTML pages to users
- Ability to **CRUD** (**create**, **read**, **update**, and **delete**) blog posts for signed-in users

If you haven't already, it is highly recommended to go through `Chapter 5`, *Building an API in Koa*. This will help provide more background information on some of the things we will do in this chapter.

 All the code written in this chapter uses the modern JavaScript ES6 syntax.

At the end of this chapter, we will have built a simple blog from scratch in Koa, as seen in this screenshot:

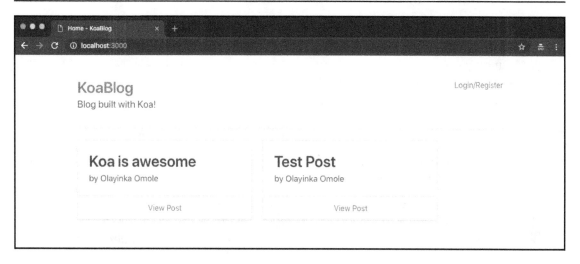

Setting up a project

As usual, we will begin development locally by initializing a project with npm. We can run the following command to initialize our project:

```
npm init
// or npm init -y
```

 Running npm init -y initializes the project with default values in the package.json file.

Installing dependencies

We will be making use of the external dependencies listed here:

- koa: Our base framework.
- koa-router: RESTful Routing middleware for Koa
- koa-logger: Development style logger middleware for Koa
- koa-body: Request body parser middleware for Koa
- koa-session: Session middleware for Koa
- koa-views: Template rendering middleware for Koa

- mongoose: **Object data modeling (ODM)** library for MongoDB and Node.js
- mongoose-unique-validator: Unique constraint validator plugin for mongoose
- ejs: Templating language for JavaScript
- bcrypt: Password-hashing library for Node

To install the required dependencies, we can run the following command:

```
npm install --save koa koa-router koa-logger koa-body koa-views koa-session
mongoose mongoose-unique-validator ejs bcrypt
```

 With newer versions of npm, you do not need to specify the --save flag for installed packages to be added as dependencies in the package.json file. You can simply install and save dependencies with npm install or npm i.

Project structure

We will be using a similar modular file and folder structure as seen in the previous chapter. Initially, we will create the following folders and files:

- controllers: This folder will house the files that will contain our application's main business logic.
- middleware: This folder will contain all our custom middleware.
- models: This folder will contain our data objects and mongoose schemas.
- views: This folder will contain the template files for our application.
- index.js: This is the entry point for our application. Here, we will initialize the application, register all the required middleware, and start the server.
- db.js: This is where we will connect to our MongoDB database using Mongoose.

To create the needed folders, you can run the following command in the terminal:

```
mkdir controllers middleware models views
```

To create the needed files, you can run this command in the terminal:

```
touch index.js db.js
```

After initializing the project, installing the needed dependencies, and creating the required files and folders, we should have the following structure:

```
├──── controllers
├──── db.js
├──── index.js
├──── middleware
├──── models
├──── package-lock.json
├──── package.json
└──── views
```

Building the application

In this section, we will build our blog. We will be able to achieve this by following the steps given:

1. Starting the server
2. Connecting to the database
3. Creating data models
4. Setting up the router
5. Setting up the views
6. Handling authentication
7. Creating controller functions

Starting the server

We will not go into much detail on this, as it was covered in the previous chapter. To start our server, we will simply insert the following content into the `index.js` entry file:

```
// ./index.js

const Koa = require('koa');
const app = new Koa();

const port = process.env.PORT || 3000;
app.listen(port, () => console.log(`Server running on
http://localhost:${port}`));
```

The server either runs on a specified port with the `PORT` environmental variable or on the default `3000` port.

To start our application, you can run this command from the project root:

```
node index.js
```

You can also use `nodemon` to start the app for automatic reloads anytime a change is made to a file in the project folder, `nodemon index.js`

Connecting to the database

We will define our MongoDB connection in a `./db.js` file. This will help keep our `index.js` file neat and allow us to keep our configurations modular.

To connect to our database, if you haven't already, create a `db.js` file in the root directory as given:

```
touch db.js
```

Then, insert the following into the file:

```
// ./db.js

const mongoose = require('mongoose');

module.exports = () => {
  mongoose.connect(
    'mongodb://localhost:27017/koa-blog',
    { useNewUrlParser: true }
  );

  const db = mongoose.connection;
  db.on('error', error => {
    throw new Error(`error connecting to db: ${error}`);
  });
  db.once('open', () => console.log('database connected'));
};
```

In the preceding code block, first, we require the `mongoose` ODM library, then we export a simple function that creates a connection to our database using the `mongoose.connect(dbUrl, [options])` method. We are creating a connection to the `koa-blog` database.

It should also be noted that we set up listeners in our database connection function. The `db.on('error')` listener is for when an error occurs when a connection is trying to be established. The `db.on('open')` listener is called when a successful connection occurs.

Now that we have exported our database connection function, we can make use of it in the `index.js` file as seen here:

```
// ./index.js

// ...
const initDb = require('./db');

// initialize database
initDb();

// ...
```

The complete `index.js` file will now look like this:

```
const Koa = require('koa');
const initDb = require('./db');

// initialize database
initDb();

// create app instance
const app = new Koa();

// start server
const port = process.env.PORT || 3000;
app.listen(port, () => console.log(`Server running on
http://localhost:${port}`));
```

The next time our application starts, we should see messages similar to this one:

```
Server running on http://localhost:3000
database connected
```

This indicates that the connection to the database was successful.

Creating data models

Now that we have a successful database connection, we can go ahead to create data models that will control our interaction with our database.

In our application, we will need two data models:

- The `User` model: This will contain the schema for our user collection
- The `Post` model: This will contain the schema for our post collection

The user model

This is responsible for handling our database interactions with registered users of our application. It will contain the following fields:

- `fullName`: This is a string value. The full name of the registered user. This is a required field, and should not be empty.
- `email`: This is also a string value. It is the email address of the registered user. Note that this value should be unique. We will make use of the `mongoose-unique-validator` plugin here to ensure the value is unique across all our app's users. This is a required field, and should not be empty.
- `password`: This is a hash of the user password. This should also be a string value. This is a required field, and should also not be empty.
- `createdAt`: The date the document was created. This can be saved as a JavaScript date object. The default value is the current date.
- `updatedAt`: The date the document was most recently updated. This can be saved as a JavaScript Date object. The default value is the current date.

To create the data model, let us create a `User.js` file in the `./models` folder, and insert the following code into it:

```
const mongoose = require('mongoose');
const uniqueValidator = require('mongoose-unique-validator');

const schema = new mongoose.Schema({
  fullName: {
   type: String,
   required: true
  },
  email: {
   unique: true,
   type: String,
   required: true
  },
  password: {
   type: String,
   required: true
  },
```

```
  createdAt: { type: Date, default: Date.now },
  updatedAt: { type: Date, default: Date.now }
});

schema.plugin(uniqueValidator);
module.exports = mongoose.model('User', schema);
```

 The mongoose reference created in the preceding code block when we require('mongoose') will be the same as the one that was returned when we initially connected to the database.

The mongoose-unique-validator plugin is used to add pre-save validation for unique fields within a Mongoose schema. After defining our schema, we export the model to be used in other places in our application.

The post model

This model handles the interaction of our application with blog posts in the database. We will keep things very simple, so it will only have the following fields mentioned:

- title: This is the title of the post. It is a string value. It should not be empty, which means it is a required field.
- content: This is the body or content of the blog post. It should be a string value.
- image: This is a link to the featured image for the post. It should also be a string value.
- author: This the user who created the post. It is a reference to the ObjectId of the user who created this post on the user collection.
- createdAt: The date the document was created. This can be saved as a JavaScript date object. The default value is the current date.
- updatedAt: The date the document was most recently updated. This can be saved as a JavaScript date object. The default value is the current date.

To create the post model, let's create a Post.js file in the ./models folder, and insert the following code into it:

```
const mongoose = require('mongoose');

const schema = new mongoose.Schema({
  title: {
    type: String,
    required: true
  },
```

```
    content: String,
    image: String,
    author: {
        type: mongoose.Schema.Types.ObjectId,
        ref: 'User'
    },
    createdAt: { type: Date, default: Date.now },
    updatedAt: { type: Date, default: Date.now }
});

module.exports = mongoose.model('Post', schema);
```

As usual, after our schema definition, we export the model to be used elsewhere in our application.

Setting up the router

Next, we will set up our router to handle routing to different pages of our application. We will use `koa-router`, the popular RESTful routing middleware for Koa.

Let's create a `router.js` file as shown, which will contain all our route definitions in the `middleware` folder:

```
touch middleware/router.js
```

After creating the file, we can insert the following content into it:

```
// ./middleware/router.js

const KoaRouter = require('koa-router');

const router = new KoaRouter();
router.get('/', ctx => (ctx.body = 'Welcome to the Koa Blog!'));

module.exports = router;
```

In the preceding code block, we require `koa-router`, and then create a new instance of the middleware and register a simple route for the index route.

Next, we register our middleware in our entry file, updating `./index.js` as shown:

```
// ./index.js

// ...
const router = require('./middleware/router');
```

```
// router
app.use(router.routes());

// ...
```

After the addition, at this point, the complete `index.js` will look like this:

```
const Koa = require('koa');
const router = require('./middleware/router');
const initDb = require('./db');

// initialize database
initDb();

// create app instance
const app = new Koa();

// register middlware
app.use(router.routes());

// start server
const port = process.env.PORT || 3000;
app.listen(port, () => console.log(`Server running on
http://localhost:${port}`));
```

Now that we have the router defined and registered, a request to http://localhost:3000 should produce a result similar to what is seen in this screenshot:

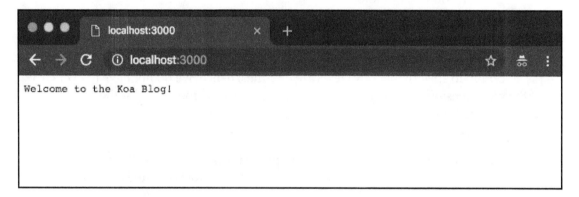

 Remember to replace the port when visiting the app on your browser if you are using a different one than 3000.

Setting up the views

To serve HTML pages, we will need to implement a view middleware and a templating engine. The templating engine will help us pass and use data from our application in our views and make the views reusable. We will be making use of the `koa-views` publicly available middleware as our template rendering middleware. We will also use `ejs` along with it as the templating engine of choice.

To register our view renderer and templating engine, add the following line to the `./index.js` file as shown here:

```
// ./index.js

// ...
const views = require('koa-views');

app.use(views(`${__dirname}/views`, {
  extension: 'ejs'
}));
```

In the preceding code block, first, we require the `koa-views` middleware. Next, we register it using the `views(dirName, [options])` middleware function.

 Ensure the views middleware is registered before the router middleware. This ensures that the `ctx.render()` method is available for use within our route definitions.

The middleware function takes the directory name containing the views as the first parameter, then an object of options as its second parameter. We pass in the `{ extension: 'ejs' }` option to specify that our views are `ejs` files; hence, we do not have to explicitly write the file extensions when using the `ctx.render()` function later. For the full list of options accepted by `koa-views`, you can check its documentation (https://www.npmjs.com/package/koa-views).

Next, let's create a simple view to serve as our application's home page. We will create an `index.ejs` file in the `views` folder and insert the following content into it:

```
<!-- ./views/index.ejs -->

<!DOCTYPE html>
<html>
<head>
  <meta charset="utf-8">
  <meta name="viewport" content="width=device-width, initial-scale=1">
```

```
  <title>Welcome - KoaBlog</title>
  <link rel="stylesheet"
href="https://cdnjs.cloudflare.com/ajax/libs/bulma/0.7.2/css/bulma.min.css"
>
</head>
<body>
  <section class="section">
    <div class="container">
      <div class="columns">
        <div class="column">
          <h1 class="title"><a href="/">KoaBlog</a></h1>
          <p class="subtitle">Blog built with Koa!</p>
        </div>
      </div>
    </div>
  </section>
</body>
</html>
```

 In the preceding markup, we include `bulma`, a popular CSS framework, to give us access to some pre-made styles out of the box. This helps to make our views look a bit prettier.

Finally, in our router middleware, we can specify that the file should be served using the now-available `ctx.render()` method as seen here:

```
// ./middleware/router.js

router.get('/', ctx => ctx.render('index'));
```

Now when we visit our index route, instead of plain text we should see the `index.ejs` file rendered as HTML as seen here:

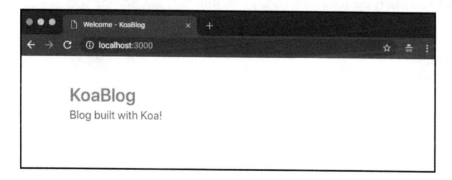

Using partials

To keep our template code reusable, we can introduce partials. We will essentially create two partials given here:

- `header.ejs`: to contain all the markup common to our application's header
- `footer.ejs`: similarly, to contain all common footer specific markup

Both partials will be placed in a `partials` folder within the `views` folder. We can create both files and place the required contents in them. For the `header` file, use the code given:

```
<!-- ./views/partials/header.ejs -->

<!DOCTYPE html>
<html>
<head>
  <meta charset="utf-8">
  <meta name="viewport" content="width=device-width, initial-scale=1">
  <title>Welcome - KoaBlog</title>
  <link rel="stylesheet"
href="https://cdnjs.cloudflare.com/ajax/libs/bulma/0.7.2/css/bulma.min.css"
>
</head>
<body>
  <section class="section">
    <div class="container">
      <div class="columns">
        <div class="column">
          <h1 class="title"><a href="/">KoaBlog</a></h1>
          <p class="subtitle">Blog built with Koa!</p>
        </div>
      </div>
```

We should also insert the following code block into the `footer.ejs` file:

```
<!-- ./views/partials/footer.ejs -->

    </div>
  </section>
</body>
</html>
```

Next, we can include them in the index.ejs file using the include helper function available within ejs as shown:

```
<!-- ./views/index.ejs -->

<%- include( 'partials/header.ejs' ) -%>

<%- include( 'partials/footer.ejs' ) -%>
```

Now that we have our views implemented, we can go ahead to set up authentication on our app to protect some of the views that we will create.

Setting up sessions

Before implementing authentication, we need to set up a session middleware for our application. This will help us store data relating to each browser session, and we will be using to store user details for each logged-in user.

To help us handle sessions, we will be using the koa-session middleware. To register it, let's update the ./index.js file as shown:

```
// ./index.js

// ...
const session = require('koa-session');

app.keys = ['secret key'];

app.use(session(app));

// ...
```

Registering the koa-session middleware makes the ctx.session object available throughout our app, making it possible for us to use it to store and retrieve session data per user.

Handling authentication

In this section, we will implement authentication on our app, to ensure that only registered users can carry out certain operations. To set up authentication, we need to implement the following:

- **User registration and login**: This involves creating views and actions for users to sign up and then log in to the application
- **Authentication middleware**: This involves implementing middleware to restrict and grant access to certain resources based on the visitor's authentication status

Before we can implement registration and login, however, we need to register our body parser plugin, which will enable us to retrieve form data. We can easily do this in the `index.js` file, as shown here:

```
// ./index.js

// ...
const bodyParser = require('koa-body');

app.use(bodyParser());

// ...
```

User registration and login

To implement user registration and login, first, we will create an `auth` page that will house the two forms that we will use for registration and login. We can create the form view in the `views` folder and name it `auth.ejs`. Insert the following content into the file:

```
<%- include( 'partials/header.ejs' ) -%>
<div class="columns">
  <div class="column">
    <h1 class="title">Register</h1>

    <form action="/auth/register" method="POST">
      <div class="field">
        <label class="label">Full Name</label>
        <div class="control">
          <input class="input" type="text" placeholder="e.g Alex Smith"
          name="fullName">
        </div>
      </div>

      <div class="field">
```

```
          <label class="label">Email</label>
          <div class="control">
            <input class="input" type="email" placeholder="e.g.
            alexsmith@gmail.com" name="email">
          </div>
        </div>

        <div class="field">
          <label class="label">Password</label>
          <div class="control">
            <input class="input" type="password" name="password">
          </div>
        </div>

        <div class="control">
          <button class="button is-primary">Submit</button>
        </div>
      </form>
    </div>

    <div class="column">
      <h1 class="title">Login</h1>

      <form action="/auth/login" method="POST">
        <div class="field">
          <label class="label">Email</label>
          <div class="control">
            <input class="input" type="email" placeholder="e.g.
            alexsmith@gmail.com" name="email">
          </div>
        </div>

        <div class="field">
          <label class="label">Password</label>
          <div class="control">
            <input class="input" type="password" name="password">
          </div>
        </div>

        <div class="control">
          <button class="button is-primary">Submit</button>
        </div>
      </form>
    </div>
  </div>
<%- include( 'partials/footer.ejs' ) -%>
```

Now that we have our forms created, let's create the controller actions for serving and handling the forms. We will create an `AuthController` file in the `controllers` folder to hold all the actions needed. Insert the following content into the file:

```js
// ./controllers/AuthController.js

const User = require('../models/User');
const bcrypt = require('bcrypt');
const BCRYPT_SALT_ROUNDS = 12;

module.exports = {
  async index(ctx) {
    ctx.state = { title: 'Login or Register' };
    await ctx.render('auth');
  },

  async register(ctx) {
    const { body } = ctx.request;
    const userData = {
      ...body,
      password: await bcrypt.hash(body.password, BCRYPT_SALT_ROUNDS)
    };
    const user = await new User(userData).save();
    ctx.session.user = user;
    ctx.redirect('/');
  },

  async login(ctx) {
    const { body } = ctx.request;
    const user = await User.findOne({ email: body.email });
    if (!user) ctx.throw(404, 'user not found');
    const isValid = await bcrypt.compare(body.password, user.password);
    if (isValid) {
      ctx.session.user = user;
      ctx.redirect('/');
    } else {
      ctx.redirect('/auth');
    }
  },

  async logout(ctx) {
    delete ctx.session.user;
    ctx.redirect('/auth');
  }
};
```

The controller created contains three methods that are given here:

- index: This loads the auth page and shows the register and login forms.
- register: This handles registration by doing the following:
  - Getting the user data submitted in the form.
  - Generating a hash of the user password using the bcrypt library.
  - Saving the user to the database.
  - Setting the user in the current session.
  - Redirecting the user to the home page.
- login: This handles user login by doing the following:
  - Getting the user data submitted via the form.
  - Retrieving a user matching the email address from the database.
  - Comparing the password supplied to the one in the database using the bcrypt library.
  - Setting the user in the current session if the password supplied is correct.
  - Redirecting the user based on the correctness of the password supplied.
- logout: This removes the user object from the session object. This means our application will no longer recognize the user as logged in.

Next, we register these actions in our router.js file:

```
// ./middleware/router.js

// ...

// we are passing the title variable to the view now
router.get('/', ctx => ctx.render('index', { title: 'Welcome' }));

const authController = require('../controllers/AuthController');

// auth routes
const auth = new KoaRouter()
  .get('/', authController.index)
  .post('/login', authController.login)
  .post('/register', authController.register)
  .get('/logout', authController.logout);
router.use('/auth', auth.routes());

// ...
```

In the preceding code block, we create a new router instance for the `auth` routes and register them as sub-routes under our main router using `router.use('/auth', auth.routes())`. This means that all the `auth` routes will be accessible under the `'/auth'` group.

We will also make changes to our `header` file to show our page title, include a link to the `login/register` page, and show the current user if the person is logged in. Update the `header` file as shown:

```
<!-- ./views/partials/header.ejs -->

<!DOCTYPE html>
<html>
<head>
  <meta charset="utf-8">
  <meta name="viewport" content="width=device-width, initial-scale=1">
  <title><%= title %> - KoaBlog</title>
  <link rel="stylesheet"
href="https://cdnjs.cloudflare.com/ajax/libs/bulma/0.7.2/css/bulma.min.css"
>
  <script defer
src="https://use.fontawesome.com/releases/v5.3.1/js/all.js"></script>
</head>
<body>
  <section class="section">
    <div class="container">
      <div class="columns">
        <div class="column">
          <h1 class="title"><a href="/">KoaBlog</a></h1>
          <p class="subtitle">Blog built with Koa!</p>
        </div>

        <div class="column">
          <div class="has-text-grey-dark has-text-right">
            <% if (locals.user) { %>
            <p>
              Hi, <%= user.fullName %>. <a
              href="/auth/logout">Logout</a><br>
            </p>
            <% } else { %>
            <p><a href="/auth">Login/Register</a></p>
            <% } %>
          </div>
        </div>
      </div>
      <hr>
```

Note that the user variable used in the preceding template has not yet been passed to the view. We will do that in the next step when we define authentication middleware.

Authentication middleware

We will be defining three simple middlewares to help with authentication. They are explained here:

- authenticated: This is the middleware that ensures a user is signed in before they can have access to a resource. We define it by creating an authenticated.js file and putting the following content in it:

```
// ./middleware/authenticated.js

module.exports = () => {
  return async (ctx, next) => {
    const { user } = ctx.session;
    if (user) await next();
    else ctx.redirect('/auth');
  };
};
```

- guest: This middleware ensures that only not logged-in users can access a resource. We can define it by creating a guest.js in the middleware folder and putting the following content in it:

```
// ./middleware/guest.js

module.exports = () => {
  return async (ctx, next) => {
    const { user } = ctx.session;
    if (user) ctx.redirect('/');
    else await next();
  };
};
```

- user: This middleware simply takes the current user in the session and makes it available in ctx.state, which is then passed to the views. We can define it by creating user.js in the middleware folder and putting the following content in it:

```
// ./middleware/user.js

module.exports = () => {
  return async (ctx, next) => {
```

```
        const { user } = ctx.session;
        if (user) ctx.state = { ...ctx.state, user };
        await next();
      };
    };
```

Next, we can register all three middlewares by updating our `router` file as shown:

```
// ./middleware/router.js

const authenticated = require('./authenticated');
const guest = require('./guest');
const user = require('./user');

router.use(user());

const auth = new KoaRouter()
  .get('/', guest(), authController.index)
  .post('/login', authController.login)
  .post('/register', authController.register)
  .get('/logout', authController.logout);
router.use('/auth', auth.routes());
```

Now we can register, sign in, and sign out of our app! Next, we will implement the different actions needed for our blog posts.

Creating controller functions

Finally, we will create controller methods for the various actions we want our application to be able to carry out. These include the following:

- `Index`: View all blog posts
- `Create`: View a form to create a new blog post
- `Store`: Save a new blog post to the database
- `Show`: View a single blog post
- `Edit`: View a form to edit a blog post
- `Update`: Update a blog post in the database

Let's create a controller file for our post actions name `PostController` in the `controllers` folder, and insert the following contents into it:

```
// ./controllers/PostController.js

const Post = require('../models/Post');
```

```
module.exports = {
  async index(ctx) {
    const posts = await Post.find()
    .populate('author');
    ctx.state.posts = posts;
    ctx.state.title = 'Home';
    await ctx.render('index');
  },

  async create(ctx) {
    ctx.state.title = 'Create Post';
    await ctx.render('post/create');
  },

  async store(ctx) {
    const { body } = ctx.request;
    const postData = {
      ...body,
      author: ctx.session.user,
      image: 'https://picsum.photos/300/?random'
    };
    const post = await new Post(postData).save();
    ctx.redirect(`/post/${post.id}`);
  },

  async show(ctx) {
    const { id } = ctx.params;
    try {
      const post = await Post.findById(id).populate('author');
      ctx.state.post = post;
      ctx.state.title = post.title;
    } catch(e) {
      ctx.throw(404, "Post not found");
    }
    await ctx.render('post/show');
  },

  async edit(ctx) {
    const { id } = ctx.params;
    try {
      const post = await Post.findById(id).populate('author');
      ctx.state.post = post;
      ctx.state.title = `Edit Post - ${post.title}`;
    } catch(e) {
      ctx.throw(404, "Post not found");
    }
    await ctx.render('post/edit');
  },
```

```
    async update(ctx) {
      const { id } = ctx.params;
      const { body } = ctx.request;
      try {
        const postData = { ...body, createdAt: new Date() }
        const post = await Post.findByIdAndUpdate(id, postData);
        ctx.redirect(`/post/${post.id}`);
      } catch(e) {
        ctx.throw(e);
      }
    }
};
```

We also need to create the corresponding template files for the needed actions. Let's create a post folder in the `views` folder to house the post specific views needed. This will contain the following files:

- `create.ejs`:

```
<%- include( '../partials/header.ejs' ) -%>
<div class="columns">
  <div class="column is-three-quarters">
    <h1 class="title">Create Post</h1>

    <form action="/post/" method="POST">
     <div class="field">
       <label class="label">Title</label>
       <div class="control">
         <input class="input" type="text" placeholder="e.g Koa is
         awesome" name="title">
           </div>
         </div>

      <div class="field">
        <label class="label">Content</label>
       <div class="control">
         <textarea rows="12" class="textarea" placeholder="e.g.
         Hello world" name="content"></textarea>
         </div>
       </div>

       <div class="control">
         <button class="button is-primary">Submit</button>
       </div>
     </form>
   </div>

   <div class="column">
```

```
      </div>
    </div>
    <%- include( '../partials/footer.ejs' ) -%>
```

- edit.ejs:

```
  <%- include( '../partials/header.ejs' ) -%>
  <div class="columns">
    <div class="column is-three-quarters">
      <h1 class="title">Create Post</h1>

      <form action="/post/<%= post.id %>/" method="POST">
        <input type="hidden" name="method" value="PUT">
        <div class="field">
          <label class="label">Title</label>
          <div class="control">
            <input value="<%= post.title %>" class="input"
           type="text" placeholder="e.g Koa is awesome"
           name="title">
          </div>
        </div>

        <div class="field">
          <label class="label">Content</label>
          <div class="control">
            <textarea rows="12" class="textarea" placeholder="e.g.
            Hello world" name="content"><%= post.content %>
            </textarea>
          </div>
        </div>

        <div class="control">
          <button class="button is-primary">Submit</button>
        </div>
      </form>
    </div>

    <div class="column">
    </div>
  </div>
  <%- include( '../partials/footer.ejs' ) -%>
```

- show.ejs:

```
  <%- include( '../partials/header.ejs' ) -%>
  <h2 class="title"><%= post.title %></h2>

  <div class="columns">
```

```
        <div class="column is-2">
        <img src="<%= post.image %>" alt="<%= post.title %>">
        <h5 class="subtitle">
         <small>by <%= post.author.fullName %></small>
        </h5>
        <% if (locals.user && (post.author.id == user._id)) { -%>
        <p><small><a href="/post/<%= post.id %>/edit">Edit Post</a>
         </small></p>
        <% } -%>
        </div>

        <div class="column">
        <p><%= post.content %></p>
        </div>
        </div>
        <%- include( '../partials/footer.ejs' ) -%>
```

We also need to update our `index.ejs` file, as shown, to show the blog posts:

```
    <!-- ./views/index.ejs -->

    <%- include( 'partials/header.ejs' ) -%>
    <div class="columns">
      <% posts.forEach(post => { %>

      <div class="column is-one-third">
        <div class="card">
          <div class="card-content">
            <p class="title">
              <%= post.title %>
            </p>
            <p class="subtitle">
              <small>by <%= post.author.fullName %></small>
            </p>
          </div>
          <footer class="card-footer">
            <p class="card-footer-item">
              <span>
                <a href="/post/<%= post.id %>">View Post</a>
              </span>
            </p>
          </footer>
        </div>
      </div>

      <% }); %>
    </div>
    <%- include( 'partials/footer.ejs' ) -%>
```

Next, let's register these actions in our router file. We will also make the index route of our application point to the index method defined previously. Update the router as shown:

```
// ./middleware/router.js

const KoaRouter = require('koa-router');
const authenticated = require('./authenticated');
const guest = require('./guest');
const user = require('./user');
const authController = require('../controllers/AuthController');
const postController = require('../controllers/PostController');

const router = new KoaRouter();
router.use(user());

// base routes.
// authentication not required
router
  .get('/', postController.index)
  .get('/post/:id', postController.show);

// auth routes
const auth = new KoaRouter()
  .get('/', guest(), authController.index)
  .post('/login', authController.login)
  .post('/register', authController.register)
  .get('/logout', authController.logout);
router.use('/auth', auth.routes());

// blog post routes
const posts = new KoaRouter();
posts
  .use(authenticated())
  .post('/', postController.store)
  .get('/create', postController.create)
  .put('/:id', postController.update)
  .get('/:id/edit', postController.edit);
router.use('/post', posts.routes());

module.exports = router;
```

To make put requests work, we need to implement a method overriding middleware. This will help us change the request method for the `post` request to update a post to be converted to a `put` request. We do this by creating a `method-override.js` file and putting the following contents as shown:

```
// ./middleware/method-override.js

module.exports = () => {
  return async (ctx, next) => {
    const { method } = ctx.request.body;
    if (method) ctx.method = method;
    await next();
  };
};
```

Then, we register the middleware in our `index.js` as given:

```
// ./index.js

// ...

const methodOverride = require('./middleware/method-override');

app.use(methodOverride());

// ...
```

And that's it! Our blog post built from scratch in Koa is complete.

Summary

In this chapter, we learned about how we can build web applications entirely from scratch in Koa. We also learned how to implement session-based authentication, implement views, and handle forms for various purposes.

You can decide to expand on the current app and implement things such as custom error handling, logging, and even the `delete` action for posts.

Other Books You May Enjoy

If you enjoyed this book, you may be interested in these other books by Packt:

Node Cookbook - Third Edition
David Mark Clements, Mathias Buus, Et al

ISBN: 978-1-78588-008-7

- Debug Node.js programs
- Write and publish your own Node.js modules
- Detailed coverage of Node.js core APIs
- Use web frameworks such as Express, Hapi and Koa for accelerated web application development
- Apply Node.js streams for low-footprint data processing
- Fast-track performance knowledge and optimization abilities
- Persistence strategies, including database integrations with MongoDB, MySQL/MariaDB, Postgres, Redis, and LevelDB
- Apply critical, essential security concepts
- Use Node with best-of-breed deployment technologies: Docker, Kubernetes and AWS

Node.js Design Patterns - Second Edition
Mario Casciaro, Luciano Mammino

ISBN: 978-1-78588-558-7

- Design and implement a series of server-side JavaScript patterns so you understand why and when to apply them in different use case scenarios
- Become comfortable with writing asynchronous code by leveraging constructs such as callbacks, promises, generators and the async-await syntax
- Identify the most important concerns and apply unique tricks to achieve higher scalability and modularity in your Node.js application
- Untangle your modules by organizing and connecting them coherently
- Reuse well-known techniques to solve common design and coding issues
- Explore the latest trends in Universal JavaScript, learn how to write code that runs on both Node.js and the browser and leverage React and its ecosystem to implement universal applications

Leave a review - let other readers know what you think

Please share your thoughts on this book with others by leaving a review on the site that you bought it from. If you purchased the book from Amazon, please leave us an honest review on this book's Amazon page. This is vital so that other potential readers can see and use your unbiased opinion to make purchasing decisions, we can understand what our customers think about our products, and our authors can see your feedback on the title that they have worked with Packt to create. It will only take a few minutes of your time, but is valuable to other potential customers, our authors, and Packt. Thank you!

Index

reference 16

P

Postman
  about 62
  reference 62

R

representational state transfer (REST) 7
request object
  about 35
  content negotiation 41, 42
  methods 35, 36, 37, 39, 40, 41
  properties 35, 36, 37, 39, 40, 41
response object
  about 42

methods 43, 44
properties 43, 44

S

server
  starting, in Koa 22, 23, 24
synchronous program
  example 17

U

user interface (UI) framework 7

V

views, end-to-end application
  partials, using 100, 101
  setting up 98, 99

www.ingramcontent.com/pod-product-compliance
Lightning Source LLC
Chambersburg PA
CBHW080537060326
40690CB00022B/5160